MOBILE
FOR
GOOD

A How-To
Fundraising Guide
for Nonprofits

HEATHER MANSFIELD

New York   Chicago   San Francisco
Athens   London   Madrid
Mexico City   Milan   New Delhi
Singapore   Sydney   Toronto

1 2 3 4 5 6 7 8 9 0   DOC/DOC   1 2 0 9 8 7 6 5 4

ISBN: 978-0-07-182546-7
MHID: 0-07-182546-0

e-ISBN: 978-0-07-182527-6
e-MHID: 0-07-182527-4

Library of Congress Cataloging-in-Publication Data
Mansfield, Heather.
  Mobile for good : a how-to fundraising guide for nonprofits / by Heather Mansfield.
    pages cm
  Includes bibliographical references.
  ISBN-13: 978-0-07-182546-7
  ISBN-10: 0-07-182546-0
  1. Nonprofit organizations—Marketing. 2. Nonprofit organizations—Internet marketing. 3. Fundraising. 4. Social marketing. I. Title.
  HD62.6.M36757 2014
  658.15'224—dc23
                                                                        2013041725

McGraw-Hill Education books are available at special quantity discounts to use as premiums and sales promotions, or for use in corporate training programs. To contact a representative, please visit the Contact Us page at www.mhprofessional.com.

For those who give generously

Contents

CONTENTS

Introduction:
The Art and Science of Mobile and Social Fundraising

To effectively use mobile and social media for fundraising, your nonprofit must understand that there is both an art and science to crafting, telling, and distributing your nonprofit's success stories online. The staff responsible for your online communications and fundraising campaigns must think and create like an artist, yet implement an online communications and fundraising strategy based upon research and the study of online behavior.

In the past the academic discipline of communication studies primarily examined how messages are interpreted through an individual's political, cultural, economic, and social lens, but today, as a direct result of the rise of mobile and social media, communication arts and science are also the study of how an individual's interpretation of online messages triggers online reactions. For mobile and social fundraisers, it helps to consistently remind yourself that behind every donation, every like, every share, every retweet, every +1, and every repin, is a human being who was inspired and thus decided to donate and support your cause. Nonprofits that combine the artful creation of content with a scientific approach to mobile and social media are those that excel in their mobile and social fundraising campaigns.

THE ART OF MOBILE AND SOCIAL CONTENT

The ability to inspire giving requires exceptional writing, digital imagery, and video skills. The foundation of your nonprofit's fundraising strategy is the capability to create website articles, blog posts, e-newsletters, status updates, tweets, pins, and text messages that evoke empathy and trigger the impulse in your donors and supporters to take action on behalf of your nonprofit. Discussed throughout this book is how the art of writing, creating, and editing text and visual content can significantly increase your fundraising success, awareness for your cause, and your donors' long-term commitment to your organization. Millions of nonprofits, charities, and NGOs worldwide are now active on mobile and social media, but it's only those that have mastered the art of mobile and social content that stand out from the barrage of emails, status updates, tweets, and mobile alerts that mobile and social donors now experience daily.

THE SCIENCE OF MOBILE AND SOCIAL MEDIA

No matter how compelling your stories and visual content may be, if your nonprofit does not actively study and put into practice the science of mobile and social media, then your stories will go unread, your photos unseen, and your videos unwatched. There is a math and science to mobile and social media, and tragically the vast majority of nonprofits do not understand the science behind the effective use of mobile and social media to inspire giving. This book was written to change that. There are scientifically proven methods for growing your website and blog traffic, your e-newsletter and mobile alert subscribers, and your social network communities. Furthermore, now 10 years into the era of mobile and social media, there are also proven tactics to increase your like, share, retweet, and repin rates. In recent years, fundraising and mobile and social media best practices have primarily focused upon online conversation and crafting a personality for the nonprofit. In this book, however, your nonprofit will be encouraged to expand beyond conversation as the primary metric to gauge your mobile and social media success. And more importantly through scientific data and analysis, we will prove why your nonprofit should do so.

MOBILE AND SOCIAL FUNDRAISING DATA AND STATISTICS

This book was written during the summer and fall of 2013. Since most fundraising data are not released until late winter or early spring, the majority of the fundraising data and statistics sourced in this book are from 2012. By the time this book is available for purchase in 2014, the first reports on mobile and social fundraising for 2013 will become available. That said, from this point forward all mobile and social giving will increase. The trends in mobile web use and online giving guarantee significant growth in the years to come. For access to the most current mobile and social fundraising data and statistics, there is a series of annual reports and studies that your nonprofit should become a regular reader of:

- eNonprofit Benchmarks Study published by M+R Strategic Services (mrss.com) and the Nonprofit Technology Network (nten .org)

- Charitable Giving Report and the Online Marketing Nonprofit Benchmark Study published by Blackbaud (blackbaud.com)

- Giving USA: The Annual Report on Philanthropy published by the Giving USA Foundation (givingusareports.org)

- Text Donation Study published by mGive (mgive.com)

In addition, for the most current data and statistics on mobile and social media demographics and use, your nonprofit should regularly read the reports published by the Pew Research Center's Internet & American Life Project (pewinternet.org) and comScore (comscore.com).

MOBILE AND SOCIAL FUNDRAISING BEST PRACTICES ARE UNIVERSAL

The best practices provided in this book are applicable no matter what country your nonprofit, charity, or nongovernmental organization (NGO) is based in. However, the communications and fundraising software recommended in this book are primarily for those nonprofits based in the United States. Since Internet search results are based upon your country of origin, while reading this book it's suggested that your charity or NGO conduct online searches for the communications and fundraising software most popular and accessible in your country. For example, to locate online fundraising software, simply search "online fundraising software," and the top results will reveal the services most commonly used in your country. With almost 200 countries worldwide and thousands of nonprofit software solutions, narrowing the list of recommended software to nonprofits in the United States was necessary and pragmatic since the vast majority of nonprofits that will buy this book are U.S.-based. That said, charities and NGOs that read this book will also gain valuable knowledge on how to use mobile and social media effectively in order to build a global network of donors and supporters.

MOBILE AND SOCIAL FUNDRAISING IS A WORK IN PROGRESS

Since 2005 I have spent an average of 50 hours a week observing nonprofits, charities, and NGOs on mobile and social media. Although in my first book, *Social Media for Social Good: A How-To Guide for Nonprofits*, I rightfully credited the nonprofit sector for pioneering social media, today many nonprofits are falling behind. Too many nonprofits are still implementing out-of-date best practices and do not understand how best practices evolve and change regularly. Most nonprofits have also not fully recognized that successful mobile and social fundraisers are exceptionally skilled professionals who need a budget for software, graphic design, premium tools, access to regular quality training, and a significant block of time to commit to mobile and social media. This book reiterates often the financial requirements necessary to be successful in mobile and social media and features best practices written to stand the test of time.

For updates on the best practices featured in this book, please follow my blog, Nonprofit Tech for Good (nptechforgood.com) and its related social network communities. Since I first began helping nonprofits use MySpace in 2005, my aspiration has always been to be useful and to be of service to the nonprofit sector. I believe wholeheartedly that mobile and social media can inspire giving and raise awareness for your nonprofit's cause, but only if you use them well and strategically. Every piece of advice in this book is a result of my own personal use of and experimentation with mobile and social media. In the process I have built an online community of more than 1 million followers worldwide who support nonprofits. I say this not to boast, but to reinforce the idea that there is indeed an art and a science to mobile and social media, and this book will teach you how to excel at both.

1

CREATE AND IMPLEMENT A MOBILE AND SOCIAL FUNDRAISING STRATEGY

The number of online communications and fundraising tools available to nonprofits today is astounding—*and overwhelming*. From selecting a content management system (CMS) for your website to deciding which social networks your nonprofit should be active on, there is a dizzying array of services, strategies, opinions, and best practices to choose from. Nonprofits with the capacity and the executive buy-in to upgrade their online communications and fundraising systems can set aside months or even years for research and implementation. However, the vast majority of nonprofits struggle to find the time and resources, or they become so overwhelmed that they avoid the process entirely.

Putting off the inevitable, however, is a losing proposition for nonprofits. Mobile and social media have advanced so quickly that seemingly overnight the online communications and fundraising strategies that nonprofits have had in place for years are suddenly deficient and inadequate. This is the harsh reality that many nonprofits worldwide are starting to understand and digest. Nonprofit technology experts and advocates have been warning the nonprofit sector for years that mobile and social media were going to transform nonprofit communications and fundraising in profound ways, but a global recession that forced nonprofits to slash their budgets and implement hiring freezes was a challenging, if not impossible, environment for upgrading their systems.

Today, with charitable giving on the upswing, the nonprofits that have survived the Great Recession are ready to move forward. At the very least, most nonprofits sense that a seismic shift in online communications and fundraising is upon us and know that they need to make changes, but they aren't exactly sure what those changes are or how to prioritize them.

The first step is having a strategic plan, and this book is meant to help your nonprofit conceptualize, write, implement, and maintain that plan. The resources and best practices discussed will keep your nonprofit from spending countless hours conducting your own independent research, and hopefully it will make the process less overwhelming and more manageable.

1

Nonprofit Technology and Fundraising

N onprofit technology is the use of information and communication technology so that nonprofits can better achieve their mission and implement their programs. In practice, nonprofit technology is the utilization of hardware and software to manage donors, volunteers, and projects; to execute web and email communications; to launch fundraising and advocacy campaigns; to participate in mobile and social media; and to sell products and tickets online. If you work for a nonprofit that relies heavily on individual fundraising, the decisions you make concerning nonprofit technology will dictate your fundraising and program success and thus should be at the forefront of your mind and your priorities as you select your online communications and fundraising systems and create and implement your mobile and social fundraising strategic plan.

ALL ONLINE COMMUNICATIONS AND FUNDRAISING ARE NOW MOBILE AND SOCIAL

There are two trends in nonprofit technology that are changing the fundamentals of online communications and fundraising. The first is the rapid shift away from content being consumed primarily on personal computers to content also being consumed on smartphones and tablets. The impact of this change is that most nonprofit websites and email communications designed primarily for desktop and laptop consumption cannot be easily read or utilized on small smartphone and tablet screens. Smartphones now outsell PCs, and it is projected that tablets will surpass PC sales in 2015.[1] Although predictions and data vary widely depending upon user demographics (country, age, education, income, etc.), it would be safe to assume that by 2016 the majority of your nonprofit's web content will be consumed on a smartphone or tablet (or a smartwatch or through Internet-connected glasses), or through social networking apps, mobile browsers, and mobile email clients. Your nonprofit has two years to prepare for this shift, but you'd be wise to own and embrace the assumption that all communications and fundraising are now mobile.

The second shift in nonprofit technology is the rise and maturation of social media. With the launch of Blogger and WordPress in 1999, LinkedIn in 2003, and Facebook in 2004, online audiences are now well familiar with social media. It's been in existence for more than a decade and has matured to become a very powerful force for distributing content, fundraising, branding, and raising awareness for causes and issues. However, the vast majority of nonprofits have embraced social media only within the last five years, but even within that short amount of time its power and impact upon nonprofit communications and fundraising is astonishing. Donors and supporters now expect nonprofit content and fundraising campaigns to be interactive and social. When you combine this expectation with the rise of mobile communication, it becomes apparent that nonprofits have arrived at a tipping point and those nonprofits that focus on upgrading their technology systems now will be well positioned to reap the benefits of the mobile *and* social web in the future.

MOBILE AND SOCIAL MEDIA *ARE* POWERFUL FUNDRAISING TOOLS

The popular misconception that mobile and social media do not result in more donations hinders many nonprofits from making the necessary financial investments in upgrading their technology systems. Unless your nonprofit specifically asks your donors what messaging tool inspired them to make their donation, it's very difficult to track and allocate specific donations to mobile and social media. Until recently, mobile and social media managers (for simplicity, from this point forward referred to as *new media managers*) had to rely solely on a combination of gut instinct and tracking metrics, such as website and blog traffic, email and mobile subscribers, and social network community growth, to prove to executive staff that their efforts were resulting in more funds raised. Without concrete proof, it's been challenging for most nonprofits to get the buy-in to hire new staff, to invest in cutting edge communications and fundraising systems, and to shift budgets and staff job descriptions toward new media.

The early adopter nonprofits that are now some of the most popular, well-funded nonprofits on the mobile and social web were given the green light to experiment and to invest financial resources long before there was any proof or indication that their mobile and social media campaigns would pay off in the end. Most often these efforts were spearheaded by an ambitious and enthusiastic millennial or gen Xer who knew instinctively that mobile and social media were the new frontier and the future of online communications and fundraising. Some early adopters initially met resistance from executive staff who feared open and social communications, but they were persistent and would not give up until support was given. Others were empowered to invest time and financial resources early on by forward-thinking executive staff who were not resistant. Sadly, however, most small to medium-sized nonprofits are still struggling to get buy-in. All over the world, it's the one theme that unites all nonprofits, NGOs, and charities—they may have the green light to experiment with mobile and social media, but only if its free and doesn't require any additional investments in staff time or training. But as the statistics below demonstrate, this is an approach doomed to failure and is counterproductive to your nonprofit's future fundraising efforts:

- Thirty-seven percent of nonprofits attribute their social media success to having executive management make social media a priority.

- Fifty-five percent of individuals who engage with nonprofits on social media are inspired to take action. Of that 55 percent, 59 percent donated money, 53 percent volunteered, and 52 percent donated food or clothing.

- Eighteen percent of all social fundraising donations are referred from Facebook.

- Twenty-eight percent of text donors give in response to hearing about a text-to-give campaign on social networks.

- Online fundraising is growing on average by 14 percent annually across all sectors.[2]

To successfully utilize mobile and social media, staff time and financial resources need to be allocated. Very few nonprofits can "wing it" on a $0 budget. As mobile and social media have matured, the expectations of donors and supporters are much higher than when winging it was an acceptable strategy. It's understandable that during challenging economic times nonprofits need to pull back financially, but as the economy recovers and nonprofit staff take a breath and move forward, it's crucial that they truly digest and understand how dramatically online communications and fundraising has changed since the Great Recession began in 2007. It's the message woven throughout this book gently yet forcibly— even if you can invest only five staff hours and a mobile and social media budget of $1,000 annually, your nonprofit must invest in mobile and social media. When you realize their power and effect upon fundraising results, you'll see that they are not a financial risk at all, but in fact, will pay off in the long run.

HOW DEMOGRAPHICS PLAY A ROLE IN MOBILE AND SOCIAL MEDIA

The demographics of your donors and supporters will have an enormous impact on your technology decisions. Five years ago having a website, an e-newsletter, and a "Donate" button was an effective online communications and fundraising strategy that could be applied to all online donors and supporters. However, as the use of mobile and social media skyrocketed, suddenly this strategy became too narrow and insufficient. Demographics such as age, race, class, gender, and rural versus urban need to be considered heavily when you are crafting your mobile and social media strategy because they will have a significant impact upon your deciding what tools should be prioritized and how financial resources should be allocated. With millions of nonprofits worldwide, each with unique missions, programs, and donor lists, no blanket statements can be made about what tools must absolutely be used, but knowing your supporters well and their preferred communication and fundraising channels can help prevent your nonprofit from wasting precious time and resources. Age, race, class, and geographical divisions manifest themselves on mobile and social media just as they do offline, and staying current on demographic shifts is crucial to ensure fundraising success.

The Impact of Age Demographics on Mobile and Social Media and Fundraising

Each generation living today has come of age with profoundly different experiences concerning mass communication, and these differences directly affect how they give to nonprofits. Seniors who came of age during the era of print media still prefer print communications and charitable giving. The same is mostly true of baby boomers; however, they are young enough to be experiencing the rise of new media in their daily lives, which consequently is affecting their life-long giving habits. Gen X and gen Y both came of age during the rise of mass Internet communications and increasingly shun print communications and fundraising, while adapting quickly to new trends in mobile and social giving. And gen Y members who will come of age in a postprint era will be connecting to causes and giving to nonprofits through technologies that haven't been invented yet. Because of the rapid speed of technological advancement, from this point forward nonprofits will have to embrace multiple communications and fundraising tools if they want to reach donors and supporters of all ages.

Generation Z (Born 2001–Present, Currently Ages 13 and Younger)
Generation Z is being born into digital technology and will be highly connected throughout their lifetime. This future generation of donors will

come of age using tablets and smartphones, smart TV, mobile and social media, and technologies not yet invented. Currently, more than 50 percent of children ages 0–8 spend an average of 43 minutes daily on smartphones and tablets watching videos, reading, and playing games.[3] As the sales of smartphones, tablets, and smart TVs continue to rise, these numbers will continue to grow, representing a trend that will define a generation. While generation Z is not yet influential on your fundraising campaigns, nonprofits that work in education, child services, and youth empowerment should be laying a foundation now for future outreach.

Millennials (Born 1980–2000, Currently Ages 14–34)

The millennial generation consists of 76 million Americans who are tech savvy, well-informed, and results-driven. Eighty-three percent of millennials ages 18–29 use social networking sites on a regular basis as do 73 percent of teens. Millennials greatly prefer smartphones over any other device and send an average of 20 text messages per day.[4] Eighty-three percent of millennials donate to charity with 84 percent of those donations being made online (58 percent of the donations are $100 or less),[5] and a whopping 91 percent of millennials review a nonprofit's website before making a donation.[6] They are also more likely to donate to a nonprofit directly from a social networking site or through text than any other generation. However, the millennial generation doesn't consider technology to be a panacea for living the good life. Milliennials also value privacy and time away from mobile and social media, reading print copies of books, and regularly visit libraries.[7]

Generation X (Born 1965–1979, Currently Ages 35–49)

Generation X gives twice as much to charity as millennials do, but as millennials mature in their career and accumulate wealth, these two generations will be very similar in their giving habits. Made up of 46 million Americans who donate approximately 20 percent of all giving in the United States,[8] this generation came of age when websites and email were breakthroughs in nonprofit technology, and they have had a love affair with the Internet ever since. As the generation that also pioneered blogging, generation Xers have adapted well to the rise of mobile and social media. Seventy-seven percent use social networking sites and they are more likely to own a tablet than any other generation.[9] Those born into generation X came of age writing and mailing checks to non-profits, but they now overwhelmingly prefer donating online in amounts ranging from $100 to $499 annually.[10]

Baby Boomers (Born 1946–1964, Currently Ages 50–68)

The baby boomer generation is often underestimated in its technology skills. While print readership is highest among boomers, in recent years they have adopted mobile and social media at a rapid rate. On average, boomers spend 19 hours a week online, and 71 percent use a social networking site daily with Facebook being the most popular.[11] Thirty-six percent of boomers ages 50 and over own a smartphone, and 32 percent own a tablet.[12] When you combine these data with the fact that boomers control 70 percent of disposable income in the United States and spend nearly $7 billion per year online on consumer purchases,[13] it is a huge mistake to believe the stereotype that boomers aren't giving online. Fifty-four percent of boomer donors still mail checks to nonprofits, but the boomers are the most generous of all generations, donating more than $47 billion annually. They are also the generation that has been driving the rapid growth in online fundraising in recent years.[14] In 2012, 58 percent of boomers donated online compared to 44 percent in 2010.[15]

Silent Generation (Born 1925–1945, Currently Age 69 and Older)

Many members of the silent generations were born during the Great Depression and World War II. In 1951 *TIME* magazine published an article, "The Younger Generation," which defined the silent generation as grave and fatalistic, stating: "Youth today is waiting for the hand of fate to fall on its shoulders, meanwhile working fairly hard and saying almost nothing. The most startling fact about the younger generation is its silence." This generation, however, is silent no longer. Those 74 and older are the fastest-growing demographic among social network users, with seniors accounting for 11 percent of all Facebook users.[16] To stay in touch with friends and family, 18 percent of senior citizens own a smartphone or tablet,[17] and high-speed Wifi is being installed in assisted living facilities and nursing homes nationwide. However, print communications are still essential for donor outreach to the silent generation. Seventy-seven percent prefer to mail checks to nonprofits,[18] but it is worth noting that the percent of those aged 65 and older donating online jumped to 36 percent in 2012, up from 29 percent in 2010.[19]

The Impact of Race, Class, Gender, and Geography Demographics on Mobile and Social Media

Danah Boyd, a senior researcher at Microsoft Research and a fellow at the Berkman Center for Internet & Society, pioneered the study of how age, race, class, gender, and geography impact social networks and online community behavior. Her research on the rise of Facebook use among white, middle- and upper-class urban youth in 2008 and 2009 in contrast to a heavily African American, Hispanic, and white working-class and rural MySpace community was ground-breaking. Since then, her research has become invaluable to those committed to diversity in technology use and bridging the digital divide. In 2012 when she was interviewed by the BBC, Boyd affirmed, "The early adopters of Web technology all thought that once we got everyone online, the Internet would be the great equalizer, but instead we've found that all of the divisions that exist in everyday life, including those by race and class, actually re-emerge online."[20] For nonprofits, this means that you have to have a clear understanding of your donors and the communities you serve so that you can make wise decisions during the strategic planning process about which communication channels to prioritize and invest in. The intersection between race, class, gender, and geography and mobile and social media is complex and by no means absolute, but there are trends that nonprofits should be aware of:

- Sixty-four percent of African Americans own a smartphone compared to 60 percent of Hispanics and 53 percent of whites.

- In households earning less than $50,000 annually, 55 percent own Android phones compared to 36 percent who own iPhones.

- In households earning $75,000 or more annually, tablet ownership is at 56 percent compared to 30 percent in households earning less than $30,000 annually.

- Sixty-seven percent of online adults use Facebook. Fifty-eight percent of its users are female.

- Twenty percent of online adults use LinkedIn. Fifty-four percent of its users are male.

- Sixteen percent of online adults user Twitter. Sixty-two percent of its users are female. The largest racial group using Twitter is African Americans at 26 percent and Twitter's user base skews urban.

- Fifteen percent of online adults use Pinterest. Seventy percent of its users are female, predominately white, and come from households earning more than $50,000 annually.

- Ten percent of online adults use Google+. Sixty-four percent of its users are male.

- Thirteen percent of online adults use Instagram. African Americans, Hispanics, and women are the most active users. Instagram's user base also skews urban.

- Of those with a liberal political ideology, 79 percent use social media compared to 63 percent with a conservative political ideology.[21]

The early adopters of social networks tend to be male, white, and educated, but over time social networks have become more diverse. Pinterest was a fascinating exception in that its early adopters were overwhelmingly female, white, rural, and from low-income households. Social networks with robust mobile experiences, such as Twitter and Instagram, are the most diverse in terms of race because of smartphone and tablet ownership trends. All that said, by the time this book goes to print these stats will have shifted. As technology evolves, so do demographics, and so should your nonprofit's mobile and social fundraising strategic plan.

UPGRADE NOW, OR BECOME OBSOLETE

Emerging trends in mobile and social media clearly indicate that a fundamental shift is occurring in how nonprofits fundraise. Interestingly enough, however, print fundraising results are up, but with a twist—

check-writing is no longer the dominant method of giving in response to direct mail. In 2012, 50 percent of donors said they prefer to give online when they receive a letter in the mail from a charity, up from 38 percent in 2010.[22] For nonprofits to be successful in fundraising, they must pursue a multichannel approach using print, web, and email communications, and mobile and social media in order to appeal to donors of all ages and socioeconomic backgrounds.

Fundraising has become more complex and time consuming than it used to be, but if done well, it can be more rewarding. And no matter what communication channels your nonprofit decides to focus on, your website's donate page is central to your success. It needs to be mobile compatible with social media integration and supported by an easy-to-manage constituent relationship management (CRM) system. Your website, email, and blog content must also take into account the growing number of donors and supporters who read your content through mobile apps (applications) and browsers. Your event promotion and management must also be adapted to accommodate today's Internet users. The fact is that every online fundraising campaign is now heavily impacted by mobile and social media, and as a result nonprofits will have to upgrade their technology systems or risk becoming obsolete. If the foundation upon which a nonprofit's fundraising strategies are based is dysfunctional, then so will be the nonprofits that depend on fundraising for survival. It's not going to be easy or free, but it will be empowering in helping your nonprofit achieve its mission, programs, and fundraising goals for years to come.

The good news is that the global economy is on the upswing and with it is charitable giving. It's a slow growth, but it is growth nonetheless. In the coming years nonprofits will be able to reallocate some of their budgets to technology and to hiring new communications and fundraising staff. With more than 1.6 million nonprofits in the United States,[23] blanket statements about expanding budgets and staff hours are problematic, but as this book will demonstrate, even the most budget-strapped nonprofits can make small investments that have a big impact.

2

Get Organized

The act of researching and then writing a comprehensive mobile and social fundraising strategic plan is an essential first step in getting organized. The process of defining your goals and priorities will help focus and unite communications and fundraising staff and motivate executives to make a long-term investment in mobile and social media. The strategic plan should be simple and flexible. Social and mobile media change so quickly that detailed, long-term strategic plans are often overcomplicated and become outdated within a year's time. To help ensure the success of your strategic plan, this chapter details a six-step process for researching, writing, and implementing a plan that can easily be revised annually while at the same time is workable and moves your nonprofit forward.

STEP 1: CONDUCT AN ONLINE COMMUNICATIONS AND FUNDRAISING AUDIT

An online communications and fundraising audit is a review of all your online communications and fundraising systems and should be conducted by the person in charge of writing and implementing the strategic plan. The audit need not be exceptionally detailed and can be completed in less than a week. The process of reviewing your current systems will give you an understanding of which systems can realistically be upgraded within the first year of your strategic plan and which system upgrades need to be postponed to the following year or the year after.

Begin by creating a list of the online communications and fundraising systems that need to be reviewed, and then create a document that lists the systems and bullet-points the pluses and minuses of each system. The purpose of the audit is to gain a greater understanding of your needs. It is not meant to be a to-do list, but rather a process that helps an organization begin to conceptualize both its short-term and long-term priorities. Do not let yourself be overwhelmed or stymied if you find that most, if not all, of your systems need to be upgraded. Regardless of your nonprofit's capacity, provided that you are organized and have a clear understanding of your needs, progress can be made.

Document 1: Your Online Communications and Fundraising Audit

Summary
At the beginning of the document write a brief summary that clarifies that the audit is a current analysis of your online communications and fundraising systems and that additional audits will be conducted annually. Clarify that the audit is a working document meant to chronicle progress as well as inaction.

Constituent Relationship Management (CRM) System
A CRM is a database that captures information about your donors, members, and volunteers and enables your nonprofit to track projects, campaigns, and events. It can be fully customized to serve the needs of your organization. However, it becomes more complicated to implement the larger your organization is and the more complex your needs are. Today's most effective CRM systems are web-hosted or cloud-based to allow for easy management and remote access. If your nonprofit is spending a lot of staff hours and financial resources maintaining and upgrading an out-of-date CRM, then it may be time to research and select a new CRM that is better suited to modern trends in mobile and social

fundraising. Chapter 5 discusses in detail the CRMs most commonly used in the nonprofit sector and how much of a financial investment is required to upgrade your CRM.

Content Management System (CMS)
A CMS is a website platform that enables nonprofits to easily publish and edit website content. A website empowered by a CMS gives the nonprofit complete control over its website communications and eliminates the need for the nonprofit to be dependent on a third party for website management. Most nonprofits will need a new website much sooner than later that is mobile compatible and that appeals to today's advanced Internet audience. When conducting your audit, a new CMS and website will likely climb to the top of your list of priorities. Chapter 3 lists characteristics to look for in a CMS and the best practices for launching and designing a new website that is compatible with mobile devices.

Email Communication Software
The vast majority of nonprofits use a web-based email publishing system for their e-newsletters and fundraising appeals. Unfortunately there is still too large a number of nonprofits that are sending mass emails via BCC. Even worse, they attach PDFs to such emails. Chapter 4 highlights best practices in email communications and fundraising. However, for the audit, nonprofits need to focus on email communications that are mobile compatible and professionally designed.

Online Fundraising Software
Deciding whether you need to upgrade your online fundraising software is simple. If your nonprofit's online donation page is not compatible with mobile devices and is not embedded inside your website, then investing in new online fundraising software is a must. Fortunately, as discussed in detail in Chapter 5, this is not difficult to do or financially burdensome. Additionally, if your nonprofit is ready to experiment with social fundraising and crowdfunding, the recommended software and best practices are discussed in Chapter 5.

Mobile Fundraising Software

Online fundraising is becoming synonymous with mobile fundraising and will be even more so when mobile wallets and mobile fundraising apps go mainstream, as is discussed in Chapter 6. Additionally, if your nonprofit decides to utilize text messaging and text-to-give software, or uses it already but finds your current software lacking in functionality or too costly, then advice about upgrading or selecting new software that best suits your nonprofit's needs and budget is also offered in Chapter 6.

STEP 2: ORGANIZE A MEETING TO ENSURE ORGANIZATIONAL BUY-IN

Convincing fellow staff to invest in mobile and social fundraising can be challenging. Some organizations have whole-heartedly embraced mobile and social media, whereas others are extremely resistant. Most nonprofits are somewhere in the middle. Thus, after completing your audit, you'd be wise to take a leadership role and organize an informal meeting to get input from key staff to help ensure organizational buy-in for your strategic plan. You should approach organizing and facilitating this meeting with enthusiasm and conviction because if there are skeptics or challenging personalities involved, your positive leadership and commitment to the organization will guide your nonprofit through the process of accepting and implementing your strategic plan. At this meeting, come prepared with copies of your audit, a one-page collection of stats that summarizes trends in online communications and fundraising, and five discussion questions, such as:

1. Mobile and social fundraising are growing at a rapid rate. Who are our donors? What are their demographics? Are we prepared for the shift to mobile and social fundraising?

2. By 2016, the majority of our donors and supporters will be viewing our website, e-newsletter, and content on mobile devices. Is our website mobile compatible? Do we have a budget to launch a new website within the next year or two?

3. Social media is maturing and becoming more time consuming to use effectively. This trend will likely continue in coming years. How are we going to keep up with the demands of social media? Whose responsibility is it? Do we share it? Do job descriptions need to be changed? Can we or should we hire someone?

4. What mobile communications and fundraising channels should we invest in? Should we launch a text-to-give campaign or smartphone or tablet app?

5. What online communications and fundraising channels are we currently using? Do they need to be upgraded? Are they performing well or poorly? Can any be dropped? If one or more are dropped, should they be replaced with another?

Depending upon your organization's culture and history, you come out of this meeting empowered, frustrated, or somewhere in between. No matter what the outcome, the meeting will give you an indication of whether you should move forward with writing your strategic plan and creating a budget. The meeting will also make accountable all attendees in the decision to invest and move forward, or not. A very common complaint among staff who are eager to embrace new fundraising tools and mobile and social media is that they are isolated in their efforts, undervalued, and not empowered to move forward. By holding this meeting, the isolation is removed, the value of your work is presented, and the power is either granted and your nonprofit moves forward or stifled and your nonprofit stagnates and falls behind.

STEP 3: WRITE A MOBILE AND
SOCIAL FUNDRAISING STRATEGIC PLAN

Once you have a better understanding of your capacity to implement your mobile and social fundraising strategic plan, allocate four to six weeks to write your strategic plan and to create your budget and a system for tracking and reporting success. If you take any longer than that, you risk losing the momentum you gained at the meeting.

Document 2: Your Mobile and Social Fundraising Strategic Plan

Overview

The overview should include two or three paragraphs about trends in online communications and fundraising. Include stats about the rapid rise in online giving and smartphone and tablet use. Consider including a quote from a thought leader about the future of nonprofit technology and fundraising.

Goals

It's important to understand that the underlying goal of your strategic plan is to raise awareness of your cause and brand by creating visually compelling, thought-provoking content that can be distributed and shared on mobile and social media. Then in turn your nonprofit receives more website and blog traffic, email and mobile subscribers, and social network community growth, which consequently results in more online donations, event attendees, and volunteers. This strategy takes a holistic approach to communications and fundraising and is often called *multi-channel communications* (see Chapter 7). It is a strategy that works, but only if your nonprofit fully embraces it and understands that its success is based upon the choices made in the online communications and fundraising systems. This section should list specific goals within a time frame of one year related to the online communications and fundraising systems listed in your audit, such as:

- Increase online donations by 30 percent.

- Increase website traffic by 40 percent.

- Increase blog traffic by 30 percent.

- Increase email list by 30 percent.

- Increase mobile list by 20 percent.

- Increase event attendance by 20 percent.

Each goal should be based on the previous year's performance and explained in one or two sentences. Then close this section with a positive statement about how achieving these goals will help your nonprofit achieve its mission and programs.

Action Items
After completing your audit, hosting your meeting, defining your goals, *and* reading this book in its entirety, you will have a clear understanding of what your priorities should be, given your budget. This knowledge will dictate how your action items should be prioritized. When compiling a list of your action items, be specific and list only those items that can be realistically achieved within one year. Each year thereafter this document should be revised and adapted for the following year's goals and action items. Again, since mobile and social media are constantly in flux, your strategic plan needs to be flexible and achievable within a short amount of time or it becomes outdated and no longer relevant. Achievable action items that support your goals, for example, would be:

- Upgrade online donation service so it is mobile compatible.

- Integrate our blog into our website.

- Sign up for Google Analytics.

- Redesign our e-newsletter.

- Launch a social fundraising campaign.

- Select a website design firm for a new website which will be launched in the next fiscal year.

Again, explain in one or two sentences why the action item was chosen and needs to be prioritized. In addition, since maintaining momentum and buy-in is important, close this section by asserting that progress on achieving your goals and action items will be reported quarterly.

STEP 4: CREATE A BUDGET

Once you have completed your audit and strategic plan documents, you need to create a mobile and social fundraising budget that corresponds to the action items you prioritized in your strategic plan. It's impossible for this book to recommend specific dollar amounts to be allocated to your strategic plan given the diversity of the nonprofit sector, but your budget will be largely dictated by the systems and services you select. The buy-in of executive staff also has an impact upon your action items and thus your budget. Whatever your budget, provided that there is one, your nonprofit can advance and achieve your goals.

Document 3: Your Mobile and Social Fundraising Budget

Your budget should be an Excel document that presents monthly and annual totals. The far left column should list your action items, and then an additional 12 columns should be inserted and titled, one for each month, where fees associated with your action items should be displayed on a monthly basis. A fourteenth column should total your monthly fees and be summed to display your total annual budget. If an action item is scheduled for September and it's a one-time fee, then display the fee in the "September" column. If an action item requires a monthly fee, then display the monthly fee in all 12 columns from January to December, or from July to June based upon your fiscal year. If fees unexpectedly rise or fall during the year, then adjust your budget. Again, it's crucial to write a strategic plan and create a budget that is flexible and can adapt to rapid changes in nonprofit technology.

STEP 5: CREATE A SYSTEM TO TRACK, EVALUATE, AND REPORT SUCCESS

In order to maintain organizational buy-in throughout the year, it is critical that you create a system to track, evaluate, and report success quarterly. Get organized and be prepared to either have quarterly meetings or send emails to key staff to report success. Success can be defined as achieving the goals and action items listed in your strategic plan. Provided that you listed realistic goals and achievable action items, there will be success.

Document 4: Your Mobile and Social Fundraising Success Spreadsheet

Your mobile and social fundraising success spreadsheet is an Excel document formatted so that success can be easily seen. The far left column should list the goals detailed in your strategic plan. Then add 12 columns and title one for each month, where the metrics associated with your action items should be entered on a monthly basis. For example, if your goal is to increase website traffic by 40 percent over one year, then the metric to track is monthly website traffic. If your goal is to increase your email list by 30 percent, then the metric to track is your total number of e-newsletter subscribers on a monthly basis. Pick one day a month and enter your metrics. A fourteenth column should then be inserted to list the numeric value of your goals. For example, if your nonprofit received 10,000 unique visitors in the month previous to the first month listed in your success spreadsheet and your annual goal is to increase your monthly visitors by 4 percent, then the fourteenth column should list a numeric value of 14,000 (10,000 × 1.4).

To effectively demonstrate your success, you will need to have access to your website and blog traffic, your e-newsletter and mobile lists, your monthly online and mobile fundraising totals, and your event attendees totals. There is a math to mobile and social media, and thus to mobile and social fundraising. Provided that you implement a multichannel communications and fundraising strategy and upgrade your mobile and social fundraising systems, the numbers in your mobile and social fundraising success spreadsheet will grow month to month, year after year.

STEP 6: IMPLEMENT YOUR MOBILE AND SOCIAL FUNDRAISING STRATEGIC PLAN

Conducting the audit, hosting the meeting, and writing the strategic plan will most likely require a lot of research and leadership skills. If you have made it this far, your reward is that you now get to implement the new systems and services that you've selected for year one and to experience daily the transformation in your online communications and fundraising. People who work in online communications and fundraising do so because they thrive on change and advances in nonprofit technology. If they have been held back in recent years, the implementation of a mobile and social fundraising strategic plan is an exciting time and for many a long time coming.

To clarify, your strategic plan thus far consists of the four documents discussed in this chapter. When reporting success on a quarterly basis, share your strategic plan, your budget, and your success spreadsheet with key staff. These three quarterly documents will change throughout the year, while the audit will be revised only once a year so it only needs to be shared annually. Throughout the first year it's important to remember that if you stay organized, the success you achieve could lead to more organizational buy-in and a larger budget for the second year.

You are not yet finished with your strategic plan. As mentioned earlier, creating visually compelling, thought-provoking content that can be distributed and shared on mobile and social media is crucial for your strategic plan to be successful. Thus your nonprofit also needs to create and maintain a mobile and social content strategy (as detailed in Chapter 7) which should be added as an addendum to your strategic plan. Eventually, as you progress into becoming a more mobile and social nonprofit, you come to realize that your fundraising plan and your content strategy are entirely interwoven and interdependent.

3

Websites

Your website is the foundation upon which all your online communications and fundraising campaigns are built. How your donors and supporters access your website is changing at a rapid rate worldwide. With Africa and Asia in the lead, 20 percent of all global website traffic now occurs on smartphones and tablets.[1] With the sales of mobile devices expected to surpass sales of PCs in 2015, your nonprofit would be wise to assume and act upon the fact that more than 50 percent of your website traffic will occur on screens varying in sizes from one to six inches by 2016. The shift to mobile browsing is happening across all demographics and will affect every nonprofit worldwide. If your donors and supporters cannot easily read your website on a smartphone or tablet, then your content strategy—and thus your mobile and social fundraising strategy—is futile.

Furthermore, search engines such as Google, Yahoo!, and Bing have changed their algorithms to lower the scores of websites that are not mobile compatible.[2] Similar to social media, the surge toward mobile is not a fad, and the longer you postpone the inevitable, the more it's going to cost your nonprofit in lost fundraising dollars and brand reputation. Donors and supporters have little patience with poorly executed online communications and fundraising campaigns. In order to stay relevant, your nonprofit must take a "no excuses" approach to mobilizing your website, email communications, and online fundraising campaigns. It's imperative that you find the funds and the tech know-how to position your nonprofit for future survival. One of the downsides of the rise in social media is that it has inadvertently resulted in nonprofits becoming overly accustomed to and dependent upon "free" online tools. This mindset is becoming destructive to the sector itself. If it's any comfort, know that today's website, email, and online fundraising tools are a fraction of the cost that they were a decade ago, but they are not free. The era of free is over.

THE IMPORTANCE OF LAUNCHING A MOBILE-COMPATIBLE WEBSITE

The increase in mobile Internet browsing has an impact on every online campaign and communication channel used in your fundraising and content strategies. If you send an e-newsletter and its read on a mobile device, but designed for desktop, then the power of your email campaign is diminished. If donors or supporters click on a link in your e-newsletter or one that you shared on Facebook or Twitter using their smartphone and the link goes to a website that is not mobile compatible, then the click-through is meaningless. Some nonprofits are very aware of this shift in content consumption and are moving quickly to adapt, but most are not. Many nonprofits think that "going mobile" will be time consuming and costly so they postpone it. But the cost of not upgrading is already revealing itself. In 2013 it was reported that email fundraising response rates had dropped by 21 percent,[3] and many immediately concluded incorrectly that the decrease was the result of email becoming an irrelevant and outdated communication channel. The reason for the drop is more likely because 50 percent of donors who attempt to donate on your website on a smartphone give up before completing the donation.[4] Reading email is the number one activity on smartphones and tablets,[5] not social networking or gaming, and thus fundraising email appeals are losing their power, not because email is passé, but because the donate page that the fundraising appeals link to are not mobile compatible. The fact that email fundraising has suddenly lost a fifth of its power because of mobile incompatibility should put to rest any argument at your organization about whether you need to invest in a mobile-compatible website. Odds are that if your nonprofit's website is not mobile compatible, then you are losing online donors regularly. With the rapid rise of online giving, it is reckless to not prioritize a transition to mobile and social compatibility.

Nonprofits with technical know-how or access to a web designer may not need to launch a new website in order to be mobile compatible. Some tweaking of HyperText Markup Language (HTML) and Cascading Style Sheets (CSS), overall site layout, and graphic design could significantly improve how your website is viewed on tablets and smartphones. However, in most cases this is only a temporary fix. The design aesthetics of mobile are usurping those of traditional desktop design so quickly that most websites designed for desktop browsing are not adequate for your long-term mobile and social fundraising strategy. You could also launch a separate mobile website and add redirect code to your desktop site so that mobile visitors are automatically redirected to your mobile site, but that may require running two different websites. A third and increasingly popular option is to launch a new website that is responsively designed. Websites that are responsively designed are built on a fluid, grid-based framework that allows for flexibility in page width and image sizes thus enabling the website to automatically convert and reshape itself to fit the browser on which it's being viewed—whether that's a two-inch smartphone screen or 17-inch laptop screen. For many nonprofits it's simply easier and more cost-effective to launch a new responsively designed website than to try to retrofit or redesign their current website.

Deciding what approach you'll take to make your website mobile compatible is the first step. You will find the best advice from a design firm or independent designer who knows your nonprofit well or takes the time to understand your needs. Be sure to be very wary of a firm or designer who is not familiar with mobile or who encourages you to build your website using an obscure CMS or design software. Sadly, and all too often, nonprofits launch new websites that are not mobile compatible, or that are built using a CMS that is riddled with bugs and glitches. Even worse and shocking to still be happening in 2014, nonprofits are launching websites that they cannot edit themselves because they have been built with outdated website design publishing software that only the designer knows how to use. Whichever method you choose, your budget, your website's current CMS, the complexity of your content, and the size of your website will have the greatest impact on your decision. Finally, when launching your new website, send out an email announcement and share your projected launch date on mobile and social media one week before launch in order to build anticipation. Never announce the launch of your new website on a weekend or holiday.

SELECTING A CONTENT MANAGEMENT SYSTEM

The most commonly used, highly rated, and free content management systems are WordPress (wordpress.org), Joomla (joomla.org), and Drupal (drupal.org). Nonprofits with tech-savvy staff can download and then host the CMS software on a server, such as Bluehost (bluehost.com), and then set up and design the website themselves using predesigned templates. In most cases, however, it's better to hire a website designer who specializes in WordPress, Joomla, or Drupal. All three content management systems offer a growing number of responsively designed templates that can be modified by your designer to match the particular needs of your nonprofit. The cost from download to launch can range from $5,000 to $25,000, depending on your graphic design needs, the complexity of the site, and how many work hours are put in by your designer. For nonprofits that simply need to be able to publish website articles, blog posts, donate pages, and an events calendar, WordPress, Joomla, and Drupal make excellent low-cost options. The CMS software itself is secure and regularly updated, and their solid reputation and use is widespread in the nonprofit sector.

For large nonprofits that need more robust websites that include e-advocacy and social fundraising, Blackbaud offers a suite of services including its own CMS and CRM. On the whole, the services are quite costly. However, there are many companies, such as Salsa Labs and Engaging Networks, that do not offer their own CMS, but do offer e-advocacy tools, social fundraising software, event and donor management services, and email communications that can all be integrated into your website by a skilled website designer. When conducting your nonprofit technology audit and writing your mobile and social fundraising plan, researching and selecting the services you need to match your goals will be the most time-consuming part of the process.

Finally, for small to tiny nonprofits on limited budgets, there are website publishing services such as Nation Builder (nationbuilder.com) and Squarespace (squarespace.com) that allow you to easily customize modern, well-designed, mobile-compatible website templates for as little as $20 a month with very little technical know-how. Nation Builder is unique in that in addition to a website, the service also offers donor management, email communications, and online fundraising services at exceptionally low monthly fees. In this Internet age, with a little tech know-how, a working budget for graphic design, and some free time, you can significantly improve your online communications and fundraising. In the spirit of tough love, it has to be said that there is no excuse good enough to continue to have a website reminiscent of the late 1990s and early 2000s. Whether your nonprofit is an all-volunteer operation or a small nonprofit of two or three staff, there are services available that can propel your nonprofit into the twenty-first century on a minimal budget.

10 WEBSITE DESIGN BEST PRACTICES

As your donors and supporters become increasingly overwhelmed by the volume of content and messages being emailed, tweeted, texted, and broadcast to them on a daily basis, the trend toward using more visual content and easier-to-process text is transforming long-held website design principles. Fortunately, these new design aesthetics make for a better browsing experience on both mobile devices and PCs. This is why responsive design is becoming adopted so quickly by nonprofits. Your nonprofit needs only one website that adheres to one set of design best practices, yet it communicates your stories and calls-to-action effectively no matter what device they are being viewed on and read.

1. Focus on Consistency and Spaciousness

Whether it's a first visit or a thorough exploration of your website, the layout and images should be consistent in size. Body content and sidebars should be the same width, and headline and secondary images should all be the same size and flow from page to page for easy processing of key messages. It's also important to provide ample space between headline stories and images for easy scanning and processing of content.

2. Use More Images and Less Text

It wasn't that long ago when home pages were loaded with text-heavy content and when images were used simply to complement featured stories. Today, the images are the featured content, and the text is used only to headline the story associated with the image. In general, no more than a headline or a sentence of text should be featured on your home page with each featured image and story, and all images should link to the corresponding article or web page. Also, your nonprofit should become skilled at creating graphics for cause awareness campaigns, events, and calls to action. For example, a text headline that asks donors and supporters to RSVP to your annual gala should be converted into a graphic with a background image and an embedded RSVP button. In addition to being more visually compelling, these graphics can also be shared on social networks which ensures higher interaction and engagement rates and thus more event attendees.

3. Increase Font Size

Responsive website design is trending toward using headlines that range in font size from 20 to 36 points, while subtext ranges from between 14 and 22 points. The body text of articles and blog posts should be at least 12 points, but be willing to experiment with 13 or 14 points. The larger your font, the easier your content is to read on both mobile devices and PCs.

4. Simplify Navigation and Don't Use Pop-Down Menus

Pop-down menus are difficult to navigate on tablets and smartphones, and a navigation bar with five or fewer primary tabs makes for a simplified, more powerful navigation experience that features your most important programs and calls to action. If your nonprofit has a complex website and creates a lot content, organize that content into subpages that can be quickly tapped or clicked through.

5. Prominently Feature a "Donate" Button on Every Page of Your Website

Since your nonprofit will often link to website articles and blog posts in e-newsletters, on social networks, and in mobile alerts, be sure that a "Donate" or "Donate Now" button is prominently featured on every page of your website. This can easily be done by creating a "Donate" tab in your navigation bar or by incorporating a donate button or graphic into your featured banner image(s) or sidebar design. Buttons should also be bold and colorful so that they draw the immediate attention of your readers.

6. Focus on E-Newsletter and Mobile Alert Subscription Forms Rather Than Buttons

The opt-in rate for e-newsletters and mobile alerts is three times higher when a form is directly embedded in your home page rather than having a "Subscribe" button that links to a secondary page where visitors can fill out a subscription form. Since email and mobile alerts are critical to your fundraising success, ensure that the subscription forms are embedded on every page of your website. This is most easily done by adding them to the sidebar.

7. Add Social Network Icons to the Upper Right-Hand Corner

Website visitors tend to digest content from center to right to left. Therefore, the upper right-hand corner is the best location for featuring calls to action, donate and subscribe pitches, and social network icons. Many nonprofits put the icons at the bottom of their website, but most visitors never scroll down far enough to reach the bottom of your website, especially if they are browsing on a mobile device. A careful inspection of your website analytics will reveal that it is common for website visitors to follow your nonprofit on social networks directly from your website, so make it easy for them to find you by featuring social network icons that are easy to tap or click and are consistent in size and alignment.

8. Use Large Buttons for Calls to Action for Easy Tapping and Clicking

When using call-to-action buttons, it's important to consider that tapping will soon be the primary means for click-throughs and opt-ins. Buttons that are 44 pixels in height are optimal for browsing on PCs, tablets, and smartphones.

9. Host Your Blog Inside Your Website

The more often your nonprofit blogs, the higher the search engine optimization (SEO) value for your website. A blog hosted within your website also ensures consistency in branding and more traffic to your website. Since blog posts are well-received and highly shared on mobile and social media, your blog should also prominently feature donate and subscribe pitches and social network icons, as well as any graphics for cause awareness campaigns or other calls to action that are currently being promoted on your website.

10. Add Social Sharing and Comment Functionality

Donors and supporters often want to share your content with their social networks. Therefore, every page of your website and all blog posts should be shareable. There are sharing plug-ins for WordPress, Joomla, and Drupal, but services like ShareThis (sharethis.com) and AddThis

(addthis.com) provide code to enable you to add sharing functionality to your website or blog and both are mobile compatible. Also, Disqus (disqus.com) enables nonprofits to add commenting functionality to both website articles and blog posts. The service is unique in that readers post comments using their social network identities thus also publishing their comments to their social networks.

ANALYTICS

In order for your nonprofit to be able to track and report the success of your mobile and social fundraising strategy, your communications and development staff need regular access to your website and blog analytics. If your nonprofit is fortunate enough to have a part- or full-time new media manager, then the manager needs daily access. For your nonprofit to gage whether your content strategy is resulting in more website and blog traffic and thus more e-newsletter and mobile alert subscribers, donors, event attendees, and volunteers, you'll need a more comprehensive set of analytics than that offered by your website hosting service. By far, Google Analytics (google.com/analytics) is the most powerful and free analytics service available. It details unique visitors and page views by hour, day, month, and year; video views; referral traffic from search engines, websites, and social networks; and reports on how much of your traffic occurs in mobile browsers and inside smartphone and tablet apps. The service enables easy sharing of the data with other staff in flowchart format or by using Excel. Additionally and starting at $9 a month, CrazyEgg (crazyegg.com) offers the same data as Google Analytics, but also features your website clicks in heat maps, demonstrates how far visitors scroll into your website using scroll maps, and visually showcases when and where visitors are hitting the "back" button or leaving the site. This information gives your nonprofit insight into problem areas in your website design and navigation. Finally, you should also run a report in Google's Webmaster Tools (google.com/webmasters/tools) to ensure that Google Search is successfully indexing your site for Google Search results.

SEARCH ENGINE OPTIMIZATION

Six out of ten Americans use Google, Bing, or Yahoo! every day, and worldwide more than 5 billion searches are conducted daily.[6] Increasingly those searches are being done on mobile devices. Mobile and social media are powerful drivers of referral traffic. However, optimizing your website to appear prominently in search engine results is still incredibly important. As mentioned earlier, simply having a website that is mobile compatible increases your search engine optimization (SEO), but your website design firm or designer will know and should implement advanced SEO tactics, such as title tags, meta descriptions, semantic coding, Extensible Markup Language (XML) site maps, (Uniform Resource Locator) URL structure, and using redirects if your new website is housed on a new domain or if old pages need to be redirected to new ones. There are, however, simple SEO strategies that your nonprofit can use every day to increase your SEO, such as:

- Write website article titles and blog titles that use your most important keywords. For example, don't simply title an article, "Go Red and Show Your Support." Rather, title the article, "Go Red in Support of Heart Health and Cancer Research."

- Publish fresh content on a regular basis. Each news article and blog post published increases your rank in search engines especially if the articles and posts are consistently growing in traffic and reach. Also, by effectively using email communications, social networks, mobile alerts, and making your content shareable, your traffic and thus your SEO should increase.

- Apply titles to images that reflect the content of the website article or blog post by using keywords so they are more likely to appear in image searches.

- Link to your own website and blog within your website and blog. For example, in a news article that discusses heart health, link "heart health" to a blog post your nonprofit has written about healthy eating.

- If your nonprofit is location-based, be sure to add your address to your website, prioritize your city and state as keywords, and claim your Google+ Local page and request reviews.

- Ninety percent of Internet users associate an .ORG web address with the words "nonprofit" and "trust."[7] In addition search engines often prioritize .ORG websites in search queries that are related to causes or issues; thus all nonprofits should have an .ORG web address. Nongovernmental organizations (NGOs) and those nonprofits whose mission and programs are related to international development should consider using the .NGO web address. At the time this book was written, .NGO had not yet become available, but you can monitor its release at GlobalNGO.org.

NONPROFITS TO STUDY AND LEARN FROM

❏ World Wildlife Fund: worldwildlife.org

❏ Sex, Etc.: sexetc.org

❏ Mercy Corps: mercycorps.org

❏ Malaria No More: malarianomore.org

❏ Best Friends Animal Society: bestfriends.org

4

Email Communications

Nonprofits began adding online donation functionality to their websites in the late 1990s and early 2000s with the hope that the ability to accept credit card payments online would become an instant and consistent fundraising source. Most nonprofits were very disappointed with the initial results. Many donors were skeptical of the new technology, and simply having a "Donate Now" button on their website was not enough to inspire donors to pull out their credit cards. It was during this era that nonprofits began to pioneer the use of email communications to increase online giving.

Launched in 1998, Constant Contact (constantcontact.com) was the first mass email communication software that enabled nonprofits to tell their stories to large online audiences and thus inspire donors to give online. Even today, e-newsletters are the greatest source of online donations as well as website traffic. On the day that your nonprofit sends out an e-newsletter, traffic and online donations spike and then lessen with each passing day until your next e-newsletter is sent out. This was true 5 years ago, and it's still true today. If your nonprofit is not publishing an e-newsletter on a regular basis, then you are hampering your own online fundraising success.

THE IMPORTANCE OF MOBILE-COMPATIBLE EMAIL COMMUNICATIONS

For years many marketing experts and bloggers have predicted the death of email because of the rise of mobile and social media, but the opposite has occurred. Email is making the transition to mobile. In fact, more email is now read on mobile devices (51 percent) than on desktop email (29 percent) or via webmail (20 percent).[1] Also interesting but not surprising is the fact that email subscription rates are increasing at an average of 7 percent annually[2] due to the rise of mobile and social media and their ability to drive traffic to websites and blogs where donors and supporters can sign up for your e-newsletter. Email is not dying. It's growing. Furthermore, every email address that your nonprofit accrues translates into $13 in online donations[3] over a one-year period. If you think this is trend isolated to gen X and older, it's worth noting that 65 percent of millennials subscribe to nonprofit e-newsletters.[4]

The shift to mobile is beginning to undermine the 15-year-long success rate of e-newsletters as a powerful fundraising tool because nonprofits are still sending out e-newsletters designed to be read primarily on PCs and linking to donate pages that are not mobile compatible. As mentioned in the last chapter, email fundraising response rates dropped by 21 percent in 2013 despite open rates increasing from 12 to 14 percent.[5] If nonprofits do not quickly adapt to new e-newsletter design principles, then response rates will likely continue to decrease.

SELECTING AN EMAIL COMMUNICATIONS SOFTWARE

ConstantContact, iContact (icontact.com), Vertical Response (vertical repsonse.com), and MailChimp (mailchimp.com) are the most widely used email communication software in the nonprofit sector, and they can be integrated with most CRM systems. Many CRM systems also offer their own email communication software. In some cases using your CRM email communication software is a better choice in terms of your budget. ConstantContact, iContact, Vertical Response, and

MailChimp consistently earn high ratings on TopTenReviews.com and always make a good choice regardless of the size of your organization. Most nonprofits know that using an email communication software is an investment well worth making, but it's tragic how many small nonprofits still use BCC for their email communication campaigns in order to avoid spending $15 to $50 a month for an email communication software. BCC emails are often flagged as spam, cannot be tracked, require manually managing an email database, lack quality design and formatting, and do not provide the tracking results necessary to gage whether your email campaigns are working. Again, a "no excuses" approach must be taken when investing in an email communication software. As the number one driver of online donations, not doing so could cost you dearly in lost fundraising revenue.

10 E-NEWSLETTER DESIGN BEST PRACTICES

It should be said that the term "e-newsletter" is a misnomer and does not reflect well how email communications have evolved in response to mobile and social media. In the early days of email communications, e-newsletters were meant to be electronic versions of your print newsletter with the same layout and quantity of content, but this is no longer the case. E-newsletters that are designed to look like print newsletters cannot be read on mobile devices and do not match today's current design principles for desktop browsing. Additionally, including large amounts of content in your e-newsletter is no longer a best practice. Most readers simply scan your e-newsletter for the most important headlines and click-through to your website, blog, or social networks only when the prompt to do so is obvious and compelling.

Often it helps to think of your e-newsletter as an e-bulletin or e-memo that is sent more often than a print newsletter would be and with much less content. Ideally, your nonprofit should experiment with sending e-newsletters twice monthly and then gage your unsubscribe, open, and click-through rates to determine if you should send them less or more often. As far as what day and time they should be sent, Monday through Wednesday and early mornings tend to have the highest click-through rates,[6] but if a surge of nonprofits began to send their e-newsletters only on Monday through Wednesday and in the early morning, then open and click-through rates would become lower resulting from oversaturation. Each nonprofit is unique and as a best practice nonprofits should experiment with days and times and use the data provided by your email communication software to adjust your strategy. Over time patterns emerge, and you'll be able to discern the best days and frequency for your nonprofit. Additionally, many nonprofits experiment with A/B testing by splitting their e-newsletter list into two or three sublists and then for each list tweak the design layout, colors, subject lines, and timing to test open-rate variation. Doing so will help your nonprofit hone in on the best e-newsletter design and timing for your email communications. The most pressing issue today, however, is for nonprofits to redesign their e-newsletter template so that it is mobile compatible and visually compelling to desktop and webmail readers.

1. Use a Single-Column Design

For many years e-newsletter design trended toward using two columns—a larger one for the body content of the e-newsletter and another, smaller column to feature calls-to-action and special campaigns. This format, however, is difficult to read on mobile devices, especially on smartphones. To ensure that your e-newsletter can be read on both PCs and mobile devices, your e-newsletter template should be one column that is 500 to 600 pixels in width and that includes a banner at the top that spans the entire width of the e-newsletter and is no smaller than 300 pixels in height. Additionally, your e-newsletter template should allow for ample spacing between headlines, stories, and call-to-action buttons to ensure ease of tap-throughs on mobile devices and processing of content on both PCs and mobile devices.

2. Increase Font Size

For easy scanning and reading, headlines should be boldface at 18 points or larger, and body text should be at least 13 or 14 points. Increased font size also increases click-through rates.

3. Increase the Size of Call-to-Action Buttons

Call-to-action buttons that encourage readers to donate, RSVP, or take action should be at least 36 pixels in height and consistent in size and color scheme.

4. Make Visuals a High Priority

Unlike desktop email, webmail, tablet and smartphone email apps increasingly automatically download email images. Thus your nonprofit should ensure that each story published in your e-newsletter includes a photo and for consistency in design, all photos should be the same size and displayed in a linear format.

5. Limit Content to Three to Five Headline Stories

Each edition of your e-newsletter should feature three to five stories that range from success stories and program updates to event announcements and calls for volunteers. The point is to draw focus to your most important campaigns and calls to action and to not feature so many stories that the reader is overwhelmed.

6. Use Short Paragraphs

Each story should be summarized in two to three sentences and include a link or button that readers can click or tap in order to read the story in its entirety. To ensure higher click-through rates for text links, bold the text and use the words, "Click to Read More" rather than, "Click Here" or "Read More." To increase tap-through rates, insert buttons with minimal text embedded, such as "Read More" or "More." As mobile email use continues to rise and will soon become the dominant method of reading email, call-to-action text links will be replaced by call-to-action buttons.

7. Add a "Donate" Button and Social Network and Mobile Alert Icons

Fundraising appeals should not be included in every e-newsletter so as to avoid the risk of your fundraising requests being perceived as monotonous which could lead to them being ignored. However, the template design should incorporate a donate button so that the option to give is always prominently displayed. And since most readers only scan your e-newsletter and often do not scroll to the bottom (especially on mobile devices), ideal placement for your donate button and social network and mobile alert icons is in the upper right-hand corner directly under or within your banner. It's also worth noting that for every 1,000 e-newsletter subscribers, nonprofits have 149 Facebook fans, 53 Twitter followers, and 29 mobile alert subscribers.[7] These ratios would be much higher if more nonprofits added social network and mobile alert icons to their e-newsletter templates.

8. Add Social Sharing Functionality

Most email communication software enables social sharing buttons to be easily added to your e-newsletter so readers can share your e-newsletter in its entirety with their social networks. Some software enables individual stories to be shared by inserting share buttons in close proximity to the stories. Adding sharing buttons to your e-newsletter can triple referral traffic from your e-newsletter,[8] so when selecting an email communication software, ensure that the service offers robust social sharing functionality.

9. Use Short Subject Lines

Long subject lines are automatically truncated on smartphones and result in lower open rates. Conversely, short subject lines result in higher open rates on both PCs and mobile devices. Therefore, when possible limit subject lines to 50 characters or less. Writing short subject lines requires creativity and skill, but doing so is crucial to the success of your email communication campaigns. If your nonprofit's open rates are low, then your email fundraising response rates will be low as well.

10. Use a Responsive Template

Only 12 percent of e-newsletters use responsive design templates,[9] but as mobile continues to grow, email communication software services will begin to offer more templates that utilize responsive design. Also, a quick Internet search of "responsive email templates" reveals hundreds of low-cost or free responsive e-newsletter templates available for download. Note that responsive e-newsletter design doesn't work on all mobile devices and is currently incompatible with desktop email clients, but that will likely change in the near future.

EMAIL FUNDRAISING APPEALS

In addition to your e-newsletter, your nonprofit should send out periodic email fundraising appeals. How often they should be sent depends upon your organization's mission and programs. If your nonprofit responds to crisis situations, then sometimes it's appropriate to send out fundraising emails once or twice weekly while the crisis is unfolding. If your nonprofit regularly responds to breaking news and current affairs, then craft and send out timely email fundraising appeals that explain how your nonprofit is responding to and serving the underlying cause related to the breaking news and ask your donors to support your efforts. Often nonprofits have campaigns that are in launch mode and need funding to secure success, or they have current programs in need of funds to continue success. In these cases email fundraising appeals should foster a sense of urgency, set a deadline for giving, discuss your program success thus far, and detail how funds can further help your nonprofit reach its goals.

When scheduling your email fundraising appeals, it's important to be cognizant of the fact that most online giving occurs between 9 a.m. and 5 p.m. on weekdays with a noticeable drop in giving during the noon hour while people are at lunch.[10] In addition, your nonprofit should prepare an email fundraising appeal schedule to tap into year-end giving.

Thirty-three percent of all annual online giving occurs in December with the last three days of the year totaling 10 percent of all annual online giving.[11] Note that email fundraising appeals also differ from e-newsletters in that:

- Fundraising appeals should be three to six short paragraphs in length and focus solely on the fundraising request. What your nonprofit says in the first sentence has the greatest likelihood of grabbing the readers' attention.

- Use emotional and powerful storytelling and personal language to inspire giving.

- Each fundraising appeal should have a unique banner image that reflects the program for which the funds are being raised.

- Include a donate button that is at least 36 pixels in height, and if your nonprofit engages in social fundraising, also include a "Fundraise" button that is the same height as your donate button. The buttons should be above the fold, that is to say, they should be visible when the email is opened. Also, all donate buttons should link directly to your donate page.

- Rather than linking directly to videos on YouTube, slideshows on Flickr, and infographics on your website or blog in the body of your fundraising appeal, create and link to a custom landing page that features the videos, slideshows, and infographics relevant to the fundraising appeal. This page should also tell the story of why the fundraising campaign is important and highlight your success thus far. Of course, this page should also have large, boldly colored donate and fundraise buttons and sharing functionality. Detailing how a $50, $100, or $250 donation will specifically help your nonprofit achieve its goals is also smart. Additionally, on the day that you send out an email fundraising appeal, post this page on your social networks.

- Ensure that your subject line communicates urgency in order to increase the open rate.

HOW TO BUILD YOUR EMAIL LIST

Not all email lists are the same. You may have an e-newsletter list that includes all donors and supporters, another list specifically for repeat donors, and another list for supporters who have not yet donated. Your ability to segment your email lists will depend on your CRM, but having multiple lists can help your nonprofit better craft your messages and fundraising requests. That said, there are proven strategies that can help your nonprofit quickly grow your email list, such as:

- Create an e-newsletter subscribe page on your website that describes your e-newsletter and how often it will be sent and promote this page on your social networks. Asking for a mailing address will significantly decrease your e-newsletter opt-in rate, but if your nonprofit has a mobile alert campaign, you should add an optional mobile alert opt-in field.

- Promote an online contest and offer free giveaways where signing up for your e-newsletter is required to enter.

- Offer exclusive content such as reports and ebooks that require an email address in order for these to be downloaded.

- Create online petitions and pledges.

- Host free webinars.

- Create and upload a compelling e-newsletter subscribe graphic (500 × 500 pixels) to social networks with a link to your e-newsletter subscribe page to better grab the attention of your followers and thus increase your opt-in rate.

- Add call-to-action overlays to your YouTube videos that link to e-newsletter subscribe page.

- Add e-newsletter opt-in forms to online event promotion materials.

- Send a mobile alert that links to a mobile-optimized e-newsletter opt-in form.

- Finally, and worth mentioning again, ensure that an e-newsletter opt-in form is prominently featured on your home page, on every page of your website, on your blog home page, and in every blog post.

NONPROFITS TO STUDY AND LEARN FROM

❏ UNICEF: unicefusa.org

❏ SOS Children's Villages: sos-usa.org

❏ ONE Campaign: one.org

❏ National Park Foundation: nationalparks.org

❏ Electronic Frontier Foundation: eff.org

Online Fundraising

Although funds raised online account on average for less than 10 percent of a nonprofit's annual fundraising total, emerging trends in online giving could radically transform nonprofit budgets within a couple of years. Seventy-two percent of all charitable giving in the United States is done by individuals with the other 28 percent coming from foundations, corporations, and gift bequests.[1] Increasingly those individual gifts are being made online. Baby boomers represent 43 percent of all giving, and 58 percent of boomers donate online.[2] Furthermore, the average online gift is $146, while the average direct mail gift is only $38.[3] A sea change in giving is occurring, and those nonprofits with the forethought and executive buy-in to adapt quickly will safeguard their future and be the best positioned to implement their programs, exude leadership, and foster social good.

THE IMPORTANCE OF MOBILE-COMPATIBLE ONLINE FUNDRAISING CAMPAIGNS

It has taken more than 15 years for donors to trust the online giving process. With the launch of PayPal in 1998 and then Groundspring (now Network for Good) in 1999, early adopter nonprofits pioneered online fundraising. Through a process of trial and error they have helped the nonprofit sector gain invaluable insight and learn best practices in how to effectively inspire donors to transition from print to online giving. Today, another transformation is occurring that the early adopter nonprofits have been quick to respond to. The online giving process is increasingly occurring on smartphones and tablets. Ten percent of donors have made an online donation using a mobile device.[4] While that number may seem low, as more nonprofits embrace mobile-compatible donate pages, this number could easily double or triple within the next two years. Knowing this, any nonprofits that do not take immediate steps to mobile-optimize their online giving process are at risk of sabotaging their programs, their staff's livelihoods, and their very existence.

SELECTING A CONSTITUENT RELATIONSHIP MANAGEMENT (CRM) SYSTEM

As online giving continues to grow, so will your online donor data. Investing now in a CRM that is tailored to capture and report online giving data will ensure that your nonprofit's donor management and communication strategies are streamlined and effective. Today's best CRM systems allow for easy integration with the most commonly used fundraising, event management, and email and text communications software thus eliminating the common practice of exporting and importing data to your CRM. Some CRM systems include a comprehensive software package in which they provide the donor database as well as fundraising, communications, event management, and accounting software.

Selecting a CRM that fits your nonprofit's unique needs and budget can be time consuming and confusing. However, to prepare for the shift to mobile and social fundraising, it's time well-invested that will over the long run save your nonprofit financial resources and countless hours in staff time administering and updating an antiquated CRM. A new CRM need not be a significant financial investment. Over time as technology has advanced, CRM systems have become more affordable and more powerful. Some CRM services charge as little as $100 a month, and others offer a one-time set-up fee of $5,000–10,000. To help in your research, Idealware (idealware.org) offers comprehensive resources and comparison guides about the CRM systems most commonly utilized by the nonprofit sector such as CiviCRM, Salesforce, DonorPerfect, Salsa Labs, Blackbaud (eTapestry and Raiser's Edge), Abila, Engaging Networks, The Databank, Nonprofit Easy, Little Green Light, NeonCRM, Corduro, and Donor Pro. In addition, SmallAct (smallact.com) offers a unique software solution that merges your mobile and social media analytics with the transaction and financial data from your nonprofit's CRM to find your donors and key influencers on mobile and social networks. Odds are that over time all CRM systems will become integrated with mobile and social media.

SELECTING AN ONLINE FUNDRAISING SOFTWARE

Tragically, too many nonprofits are making unwise online fundraising software decisions based on saving pennies rather than raising dollars. Opting for software that offers low donation processing rates and no monthly fees, such as PayPal, initially seems like a wise choice. However, an analysis of over 40,000 online fundraising campaigns revealed that nonprofits who have the donation process within their own website raise six times more dollars online on an annual basis than those nonprofits that send their donors to a third-party website.[5] Online giving is often impulsive, and if a donor experiences confusion as to why they are being sent to PayPal to make a donation (and often prompted to create a PayPal account to do so), many online donors will drop out of the process. Also, exceptionally low-cost vendors tend to not offer many of the functionalities required today to maximize online fundraising success, such as:

- Custom-branded "Donate" pages that are mobile compatible.

- Custom-branded "Thank you" landing pages that are mobile compatible.

- Automatic, customizable "Thank you" emails that are mobile compatible.

- Recurring donation capability to enable monthly giving campaigns.

- Ability to donate in someone else's name to enable tribute giving campaigns.

- Ability for donors to share their donation with their social networks.

- Ability to be integrated with your CRM.

Most comprehensive CRM systems have upgraded their fundraising software to include all the above mentioned functionalities. If your nonprofit wants to use an online fundraising software separate from your CRM, then ensuring that the software can be integrated with your CRM through an application programming interface (API) allows for easy updates to your donor database. For example, DonationPay (donation pay.com) will integrate with CiviCRM and Salesforce through its API and offers excellent, low-cost online fundraising software. At less than $50 a month, DonationPay allows for the customization of up to four mobile-compatible donate pages as well as thank-you landing pages and emails. A nonprofit could set up one page for general online giving, one for monthly giving, one for tribute giving, and another as a paid event registration page. For nonprofits that don't mind importing and exporting donor data to their CRM, there's also StayClassy.org and Network for Good. For $100 a month, StayClassy offers custom-branded social fundraising and event fundraising campaigns. The online fundraising software you select is the most important decision you'll make when implementing your mobile and social fundraising plan. To maximize fundraising success your nonprofit must be willing to invest a minimum of $50 to $100 a month and pay a 3 to 5 percent donation processing fee.

FIVE CHARACTERISTICS OF ONLINE DONORS

By understanding what motivates donors to give online, your nonprofit will be better equipped to craft and implement a mobile and social media content strategy that ensures online fundraising success. Increasingly, online donors are inspired by the cause(s) that a nonprofit advocates for rather than the brand name of the nonprofit. Through the effective use of storytelling intermingled with marketing and fundraising content, you can galvanize your donors to give more generously and more often.

1. Success

Your donors want to know that their financial support is having an impact in helping you accomplish your mission and programs. If your nonprofit reaches a program milestone, then write a website article or blog post that chronicles your success and include photos, videos, and infographics that showcase the communities or causes served. In fundraising appeals don't be afraid to cheer your achievements, but also ensure that you communicate that your success would not have been possible without your donors' support. Donors want to read and are inspired by good news, and they want evidence that their donations are working. If your nonprofit has programs in various locations, you can showcase your success to donors by creating online maps using Google Maps (google.com /maps), Uencounter.me, or ZeeMaps (zeemaps.com).

2. Urgency

Many donors are motivated to give in times of crisis. A crisis can range from a natural disaster to pending changes in public policy. Enlisting your donors to fund your cause in a time of crisis has consistently proven to increase online donations. The trick is to communicate the dire need for donations with a tone of authority and expertise rather than opportunity. You need to ensure that your donors understand that your nonprofit is in a position to respond to the crisis. Otherwise your donors will assume that you are taking advantage of a crisis for selfish reasons.

3. Altruism

Like those individuals who choose a career in the nonprofit sector, online donors are also driven by a desire to make a difference in the world. Quite often it's easy for nonprofit staff and donors to lose sight of the fact that we are making a difference because of a 24/7 news cycle that places a high priority on negative and sensational content. By consistently championing your cause and informing donors that by donating to your nonprofit they are making a difference, you can effectively tap into the altruist tendencies of your donors.

4. Connection

Another motivating factor in online giving is the donor's personal connection to a cause. For example, if donors grew up in poverty, then they are more likely to support organizations working to alleviate poverty. If donors have a family member who died of cancer, then they are more likely to give to cancer research organizations. When you create fundraising campaigns that focus on your donor's empathy for your cause, donors with a personal connection to your cause tend to be more loyal over the long term.

5. Reciprocity

In addition to the feeling of doing something good, some donors also appreciate receiving a tangible gift in return for their donation, such as a tote bag, calendar, or book. Reciprocity fundraising campaigns are particularly successful during the holiday season. Although challenging for small nonprofits who may not have the capacity to buy and distribute gifts, all nonprofits can offer symbolic gifts during the holiday season where the gift recipient receives an email or a card describing the impact of the gift donation made in their honor—for example, school supplies donated, meals provided to the hungry, or vaccinations given to children living in poverty in developing nations.

10 ONLINE FUNDRAISING
BEST PRACTICES

Unknowingly, many nonprofits have an online donation process that doesn't appeal to their online donors. Text-heavy donate pages that bombard donors with multiple messages or prompt the donor to answer numerous questions are outdated practices that can significantly hamper the success of your online fundraising campaigns. If your content strategy is effectively inspiring donors and supporters to click on your donate button, then to maximize your online donation conversion rates, your donate page should adopt modern design and layout best practices, such as those discussed below.

1. Ensure that the Online Donation Process Fits on One Page

The impulse to donate can be fleeting if your donate process requires that donors click-through multiple pages and provide information beyond primary contact and credit card information and the donation amount. The donation process should be as easy as possible and focus on simplicity and speed. Also, at the bottom of your donate page, ensure that there is a large "Submit" or "Donate Now" button.

2. Give Visuals Higher Priority than Content

Your donate page should have a powerful banner image and one motivational paragraph across the top. The headline font should be large and bold while body content and donation form text and fields should be at least 14 points. The purpose of your donate page is to inspire donors and supporters to complete the process without hesitation by making your page and the calls to action digestible within seconds.

3. Set Default Donation Amounts

The vast majority of nonprofits do not set default donation amounts on their donate pages even though setting a default donation amount has proven to increase total dollars raised. For example, set up recommended donation amounts, such as $25, $50, $100, and $250, and have the $25 set as the default donation amount. A donor who was going to give only $15 may then give $25, and donors who want to give more and who have more to give will select a higher donation amount. It's also a best practice to include an empty field where donors can enter any donation amount. Knowing the ideal donation default amount for your nonprofit will require that you analyze your donor data to determine the donation amount that is most often given to your nonprofit.

4. Add an Optional Mobile Alert Opt-In Field

Requiring donors to provide their phone number when making a donation will result in some donors dropping out of the process. They fear you will start invading their privacy with telemarketing calls. Thus your nonprofit should not ask for a donor's phone number unless your nonprofit has a mobile alert campaign. In this case you can add a mobile phone number field that is not required where donors can enter their mobile phone number and select a tick box to subscribe to your mobile alerts.

5. Add Charity Rating Graphics

If your nonprofit has been reviewed by Charity Navigator (charity navigator.org), the BBB Wise Giving Alliance (bbb.org/us/charity), or GiveWell (givewell.org) and your reviews are good, then of course add your rating badges to your donate page. If your nonprofit is too small or does not qualify to be reviewed by Charity Navigator, the BBB Wise Giving Alliance, or GiveWell, then create an account on GreatNonprofits (greatnonprofits.org) and ask your donors to rate and review your nonprofit. You also want to regularly monitor your ratings and reviews on

GuideStar (guidestar.org). Once your nonprofit has built up your user-generated ratings and reviews on GreatNonprofits and GuideStar, then add those badges to your donate page.

6. Include Program Versus Operating Expense Graphics

Provided that your program versus operating expense ratio is low, create a simple pie chart graphic that shows your low fundraising and operating costs. There is a growing movement against low overhead as the primary indicator of a nonprofit's effectiveness. The Overhead Myth Campaign (overheadmyth.com) advocates that nonprofits cannot be successful in achieving their programs if they cannot invest in highly qualified staff members and technology.

7. Include Giving Impact Statements

Donors respond well to statements that clarify the impact of their individual donations. For example, you can say that a $50 donation helps three cats receive spay/neuter surgery or that a $10 donation provides 10 meals at a homeless shelter. Adding impact statements helps donors see how they are making a difference and can increase their donation amount or result in repeat donations. It's worth converting your impact statements into graphics or images that can be shared on mobile and social media to increase online giving.

8. Encourage Tribute Giving

Allowing your donors to make a donation in honor of a friend or loved one is a growing fundraising trend. Particularly popular with baby boomers and the silent generation, of which one-third have made tribute gifts,[6] a donation page specifically for tribute giving should be added to your online fundraising strategy. Many nonprofits add this option to their donate pages only in a pop-down menu. But to effectively promote tribute giving during the holidays or in lieu of wedding or graduation gifts, your nonprofit should have a separate tribute giving donation page.

9. Feature Monthly Giving

Often referred to as *sustainer programs*, monthly giving is the fastest growing trend in online fundraising with an annual growth rate of 27 percent.[7] In fact, some nonprofits now have two donate buttons on their website's home page—a "Donate Now" button and a "Donate Monthly" button. Other nonprofits simply offer the monthly giving option in a pop-down menu along with the option to give a tribute gift. Either way, to effectively promote your monthly giving programs in print materials, in email communications, and on mobile and social media, you should have a separate donation page for monthly giving. Also, to increase the retention rate of monthly donors, be sure to thank them at least three times annually for their ongoing support.

10. Create a "More Ways to Give" Page

In addition to your donate page, you should also have a "More Ways to Give" page that lists your tribute giving and monthly giving programs, planned giving, workplace giving, corporate giving, and so on. Be sure to also include instructions on how to give by mail or phone. Your donate page should only include information on how to give online.

ONLINE DONOR THANK-YOU COMMUNICATIONS

Despite the rise of mobile and social media, most nonprofits have not upgraded their online donor thank-you process. Most "Thank You" landing pages (the donation confirmation page) are overloaded with small-sized text and are completely devoid of creativity. It's almost as if the thank-you landing page was set up a decade ago and no one has taken a look at it since. There is no other time when you have such undivided attention from your online donors—from the moment when they submit their donation to when the donation confirmation page appears on their screen—and your nonprofit should take advantage of that opportunity to express gratitude and convert your online donors into social network followers, fundraisers, and mobile alert subscribers.

The same is true for follow-up thank-you emails. Most include jargony thank-you language and are devoid of visuals. Donors open these emails to confirm that their donation was processed, and they save them for tax reasons. If your nonprofit doesn't make a habit of donating to itself at least twice a year so you can study and experience for yourself the impression that your thank-you process is making upon your donors, then please do so as soon as possible. You will likely discover that your online donor thank-you communications are in need of improvement and are not being adapted to modern best practices, such as:

- Add social network and mobile alert icons to your thank-you landing page and follow-up emails.

- Add a thank-you video or slideshow to your landing page and follow-up emails.

- Thank-you emails should include your nonprofit's branding.

- Encourage donors to share their donation with their social networks.

- Encourage donors to also fundraise for your nonprofit.

- Include a poll that asks which communication tool prompted the donor to give; for example, e-newsletter, Facebook, Twitter, a text message.

- Create a form that asks donors to submit their social network profiles so you can follow them.

- Create an annual thank-you and program achievement infographic and include it in your donor thank-you communications.

- Use a service like Prezi (prezi.com) to create an online presentation that features program success and expresses gratitude to the donors who helped make the success possible. Then include the presentation in your donor thank-you communications.

- To make a powerful impression in a digital age, send handwritten thank-you notes or postcards to online donors who give over $250.

SOCIAL FUNDRAISING

Social fundraising, often referred to as peer-to-peer fundraising or friend-to-friend fundraising, utilizes both the power of your donors' and supporters' personal connections and mobile and social media. By enabling your most committed donors and supporters to fundraise on your behalf, your nonprofit can significantly increase your donor database and consequently your online fundraising success. Most popular with gen Xers and millennials, the average donation for social fundraising campaigns is $44, while individual fundraisers bring in an average of $219 for the nonprofit if they are first-time fundraisers and $416 if they are multiyear fundraisers.[8]

There are two types of social fundraising campaigns. The first is event social fundraising in which your supporters run a marathon or join a walk on behalf of your nonprofit to raise money for your cause. This type of social fundraising campaign is most commonly used by health organizations to raise awareness and funds for research. The other type of social fundraising campaign is when your supporters request that their friends and family donate to your nonprofit for their birthday or wedding, or they decide to fundraise for a nonprofit when a crisis is unfolding or simply because they are strongly connected to your cause. For your nonprofit to launch either type of social fundraising campaign, you must first select a social fundraising software. The company you choose for your CRM and online fundraising software may also offer social fundraising software at a low cost that matches the branding of your website, but there is also Razoo (razoo.com), Qgiv (qgiv.com), CauseVox (causevox.com), Causes (causes.com), and Artez Interactive (artez.com), all of which are mobile compatible.

The success of social fundraising campaigns is highly dependent upon how well nonprofits promote their campaigns and train their social fundraisers. Your nonprofit will need to have a "Fundraise" button created and added to your website, and your social fundraising campaigns should be listed on your "More Ways to Give" page. If your social fundraising campaigns will be focused on events, then integrate your campaigns into all event promotion materials. It's also important to create sidebar graphics for your blog and call-to-action images and graphics so that you can effectively promote your social fundraising campaigns on mobile and social media. You should also promote your social fundraising campaigns in your email communications. Social fundraising campaigns require a focused effort and generally need to have a high priority in your mobile and social fundraising plan for them to be successful. Additionally, your nonprofit should:

- Select a social fundraising software that has a modern design, is mobile compatible, and offers social sharing functionality to appeal to gen Xers and millennials.

- Create a fundraising guide for your fundraisers that details how to create a fundraising page and provides tips and sample copy for promoting their campaigns via email and on mobile and social media. With 18 percent of all social fundraising donations coming directly from Facebook, be sure to offer detailed advice on how your fundraisers can promote their fundraising campaigns to their Facebook friends. You should also provide them with example thank-you emails and suggest that they select achievable fundraising goals, such as $500 or $1,000.

- Encourage fundraisers to donate at least $10 to $50 to their own fundraising campaign before they start the promotion of their campaign. Many of their friends and family will hesitate to donate if "$0 Raised" is displayed.

- Offer contests that reward the fundraisers who raise the most funds during the campaign.

- Create an email list solely for fundraisers and throughout the year keep them updated on the causes that they raised money for. Since multiyear fundraisers are the most successful, sending them quarterly progress reports and thanking them often is necessary to ensure that they fundraise for your nonprofit in the future. It's also worth noting that the average individual gift for a multiyear fundraiser is $69 versus $49 for a first-time fundraiser.[9]

- Create a mobile list for fundraisers and occasionally text them fundraising tips and event updates.

- Send a follow-up thank-you email to donors with your nonprofit's branding and request that they subscribe to your e-newsletter and include links to your social networks (this email should be sent in addition to the automated thank-you email sent by the social fundraising software). After the event or campaign is over, follow up with a second email letting donors know how the funds have been used or will be used, and again ask that they subscribe to your e-newsletter and follow you on social networks.

CROWDFUNDING

Crowdfunding is similar to social fundraising in that multiple people donate publicly to crowdfunding campaigns; however, crowdfunding is focused on funding specific projects rather than individuals fundraising for their favorite nonprofits. For example, a nonprofit can create a crowdfunding campaign to raise funds to build a community garden, buy musical instruments for a school, or even launch a new website. Indiegogo (indiegogo.com) and Kickstarter (kickstarter.com) are the most well-known crowdfunding sites, but there are crowdfunding services specifically tailored for the nonprofit sector, such as CrowdRise (crowd rise.com) and Fundraise.com, which are both mobile compatible, and Fundly (fundly.com), which is mobile compatible and offers a mobile app. That said, the line between social fundraising and crowdfunding is beginning to blur. Many social fundraising services are now opting to call themselves crowdfunding services, while some crowdfunding services now also enable social fundraising for crowdfunding projects, but for the sake of strategy, it is important to understand that crowdfunding is meant for raising funds for specific projects.

Launching a crowdfunding campaign is a simple way for nonprofits to add creativity and variety to their online fundraising campaigns. Even if you are a small nonprofit, you should experiment with at least one crowdfunding campaign to see if your donors react more generously when supporting a specific project. To maximize crowdfunding success, your nonprofit should:

- Select a crowdfunding service that has a modern design, is mobile compatible, and offers social sharing functionality. Also, research very carefully the donation processing fees because some services have fees as high as 10 percent of the donation amount.

- Write a five- to six-paragraph project summary that communicates the goals of the project and when the project will begin once it's funded. Your project summary should also mention that donors will be sent regular progress reports.

- Upload a video or images that make the project more enticing to fund.

- Never begin the promotion of your crowdfunding campaign with "$0 Raised," even if you have to donate $100 to your own nonprofit.

- Integrate your crowdfunding campaigns with your e-newsletter and email fundraising appeals.

- Create sidebar graphics for your blog and call-to-action images to promote your crowdfunding campaigns on mobile and social media.

- Add your crowdfunding campaigns to your "More Ways to Give" page.

- Send a follow-up thank-you email with your nonprofit's branding and request that donors follow your nonprofit on social networks and subscribe to your mobile alerts.

NONPROFITS TO STUDY AND LEARN FROM

❑ Partners in Health: pih.org

❑ Feeding America: feedingamerica.org

❑ American Cancer Society: cancer.org

❑ African Wildlife Foundation: awf.org

❑ charity: water: charitywater.org

Mobile Fundraising

The first text-to-give campaign in the United States was the United Way of America's "Text FIT" campaign during the Super Bowl on February 3, 2008, which raised $10,000. However, it wasn't until 2010 when donors gave more than $35 million over a three-week period in response to the Haiti earthquake that nonprofits began to take text-to-give seriously. Throughout 2011 and 2012 numerous early adopter nonprofits began to experiment with text-to-give campaigns with mixed results. Crisis response organizations such as the American Red Cross and UNICEF have raised millions through text giving, but less well-known nonprofits whose missions are not related to responding to crisis situations have struggled to learn how to effectively promote their text-to-give campaigns.

The problem was that many nonprofits rushed to offer a text-to-give donation option to their donors without having thought first about an overall mobile fundraising strategy. Like all new communications and fundraising technologies, there's an initial learning curve that eventually reveals best practices through a process of trial and error. In the years since the Haiti earthquake disaster, early adopter nonprofits have learned that successful text-to-give campaigns require a mobile-compatible website, the ability to send mobile alerts, a comprehensive social media strategy, a clear understanding of what motivates text-to-give donors, and, in terms of crisis response, access to media outlets and celebrities.

As nonprofits have become more skilled at promoting their text-to-give campaigns, text giving has emerged as a viable giving method for donors, especially gen Xers and millennials—and not only during times of crisis. When you consider that it took 15 years for donors to trust and adopt online giving in large numbers, the adoption curve for text-to-give has been much shorter. With almost $100 million given to date, a shift in perception about text giving on the part of donors has occurred that makes it more likely that nonprofits can succeed in raising funds via text provided that they adopt current best practices and continue to improve their text-to-give campaigns.

THE IMPORTANCE OF MOBILE FUNDRAISING CAMPAIGNS

To many nonprofits, text-to-give campaigns have become synonymous with mobile fundraising. When you mention mobile fundraising, the automatic default is to think of text giving, but mobile fundraising can no longer be that narrowly defined. Because of the rapid adoption of mobile devices, all online fundraising campaigns are now mobile. Mobile fundraising apps and mobile wallets are on the verge of going mainstream and will have a profound impact on how nonprofits raise funds. The truth is that mobile fundraising is in its infancy, and it's unclear how it will evolve and effect our mobile and social fundraising strategies. The first step into mobile fundraising is to mobilize your website, email communications, and online fundraising campaigns. Beyond that, the next few years will be spent experimenting. Text-to-give technology and how it works will continue to evolve. It could become integrated with mobile apps and mobile wallets—or not. And there are future mobile fundraising technologies that even today's brightest, most forward-thinking new media managers can't yet conceptualize. Mobile communications and fundraising will be transformative, and those nonprofits that are willing to take part in the experiment will benefit the most. Those nonprofits that were slow to adopt social media now struggle with communications and fundraising success. The wait-and-see approach didn't work with social media, and it's definitely not going to work in a mobile Internet age.

SELECTING A
TEXT-TO-GIVE SOFTWARE

The most well-known text-to-give software is mGive (mgive.com). As the company responsible for bringing text giving to the United States, its technology is comprehensive, and the company is committed to helping nonprofits succeed. Other companies include MobileCause (mobile cause.com), Mobile Commons (mobilecommons.com), Give by Cell (givebycell.com), Connect2Give (connect2give.com), and Text2Give (text2give.com). Their fees range from $200 to $500 monthly for mobile alert and text-to-give services. Donations are processed first through the mobile carriers and then sent to the Mobile Giving Foundation (mobilegiving.org) which sends the funds to nonprofits within 30 days. All these companies offer packages that include only mobile alert campaigns and not text giving, and the monthly fees are significantly lower. If your nonprofit wants to use text messaging to send donation reminders (linking to your mobile-compatible donate page), advocacy alerts (linking to mobile-compatible petitions), or simply event reminders, organize volunteers and activists, and send other urgent calls to action related to breaking news or current affairs, then the spectrum of nonprofits that should consider using one of these software solutions widens greatly. In 2013, 33 percent of mobile users said they would like to receive information about volunteering via text, while 19 percent said the same about receiving program updates. These numbers grow each year.[1] Text messages currently have an open rate of 97 percent of which 85 percent are opened within the first 15 minutes of delivery.[2] For nonprofits eager to take the next step in their mobile communications campaigns but that are not interested in offering text giving, mobile alert campaigns are growing in their appeal and are especially effective for nonprofits that want to engage gen Xers and millennials.

FIVE CHARACTERISTICS OF
TEXT-TO-GIVE DONORS

Donors who have embraced text giving have unique characteristics that nonprofits need to be aware of in order to be effective in launching and maintaining their text-to-give campaigns. While storytelling over an extended period of time is the driving force behind successful online fundraising campaigns, text donors are often inspired to donate as a result of real-time communications and immediate calls to action. Building a database of repeat text-to-give donors is a challenge, but it can be done provided that nonprofits understand that text donors are unlike any donor nonprofits have ever experienced.

1. Impulsive

Seventy-three percent of text donors make their donations on the same day that they hear about a text-to-give campaign.[3] This is likely the result of the fact that the most successful text-to-give campaigns respond immediately to crisis situations and breaking news and current affairs. The impulse to give via text is fleeting in much the same way that most news stories have momentum and buzz for only a day or two.

2. High Tech

Seventy-six percent of text donors do not conduct much in-depth research about a nonprofit before making a text donation.[4] In addition to giving impulsively, they also initially embrace text giving without much thought to how the technology works or if it's secure. This fact says a lot about how text donors tend to trust and embrace mobile technology in both their work and personal lives.

3. Young

Sixty-two percent of text donors are either gen Xers or millennials,[5] and this is of course the result of the rapid adoption rate of smartphones by those generations. The age of text donors will likely become more balanced over the next few years as increasing numbers of seniors become comfortable with mobile technology. It should also be pointed out that 70 percent of text donors are female.[6]

4. Social

Sixty-seven percent of text donors first hear about text-to-give campaigns from TV and radio, but social networks are beginning to reveal themselves as powerful drivers of text donations. Twenty-eight percent of text donors give in response to hearing about a text-to-give campaign on social networks now surpassing events which are at 19 percent.[7]

5. Well-Educated

Seventy-six percent of text donors have completed undergraduate or graduate school.[8] They are well-informed and socially aware. This is a technologically advanced and intellectual donor base that nonprofits need to cultivate with creativity and innovation.

10 TEXT-TO-GIVE BEST PRACTICES

Text-to-give best practices focus on triggering the impulse for donors to pull out their smartphones, tap in a short code and keyword, and then confirm their donation via a reply text. When text to give first became popular, the act of text giving was a novelty and this fact alone appealed to many first-time text donors who wanted to be a part of the new phenomenon in giving. However, in order to sustain their interest in text giving requires nonprofits to invest in a long-term strategy. Text giving must be integrated into a nonprofit's overall communications and fundraising strategy for it to result in repeat donations. Unfortunately text-to-give campaigns are still too often launched and promoted in isolation from other fundraising campaigns. If your nonprofit is going to invest in text-to-give software, then for it to work you must almost invest time and additional financial resources for the promotion of your text-to-give campaigns. Many nonprofits in the early days gave up their campaigns too soon because of poor results, but had the best practices that exist now existed then, fundraising success would likely not have been so elusive.

1. Launch a Mobile Alert Campaign

Individuals who subscribe to your mobile alerts are some of your most committed donors and supporters. The fact that the vast majority open your mobile alert within 15 minutes of delivery requires nonprofits to consider very carefully how this select group of individuals is different from your e-newsletter subscribers and social network followers. Every message that you send to the donors on your mobile list should be strategic and take into account the characteristics that define text donors; that is, they're smart, well-informed, young, and tech savvy. They want useful information and periodic calls to action. In addition they want to be sent fundraising pleas only when they are urgent. It's best to think of your mobile alert subscribers as an on-call mobile community that your nonprofit can activate when a situation arises that requires immediate action. Some nonprofits even refer to their mobile alert subscribers as a "mobile action network."

Since most urgent situations are unpredictable, you can't schedule mobile alerts months or even weeks in advance. Sending an average of two texts per month is a good starting point for your campaign. You can then adjust the frequency based upon your unsubscribe rates and click-throughs (monitor your website analytics). Note that not all mobile alerts need to be urgent. They can be event reminders, calls for volunteers, or announcements of new programs. There's also the occasional marketing text that can be sent requesting that subscribers sign up for your nonprofit's e-newsletter and follow you on social networks. One thing is certain, however. If you don't have a mobile-compatible website, you are not ready for a mobile alert campaign. There's no point in texting a desktop link to a smartphone. Finally, when sending an urgent text-to-give request to your subscribers, make the donation process as simple as possible. Rather than asking subscribers to text a keyword to a short code (e.g., Text WOLVES to 70505 to donate $10 to NWF), simply ask them to reply to your mobile alert (Reply WOLVES to donate $10). Eliminating the need to create a new text message to donate makes it more likely that impulsive donors will reply and give.

2. Build Your Mobile List Online

Unfortunately text-to-give donors cannot be automatically subscribed to your mobile list, which makes it challenging to follow up with text donors. Strict antispam laws require individuals to opt in to mobile alerts in the same way that they make a text donation—by sending a keyword to a short code and then confirming their subscription in a reply text or by entering their mobile number into an opt-in field on your website to receive a subscription confirmation text. Thus, to effectively build your mobile list, your nonprofit needs to integrate your mobile alert campaign with all communications. The best way to build your mobile list online is to create a mobile opt-in page on your website that describes your mobile alert campaign and includes a mobile opt-in form. You can then promote the page in your email communications, on your blog, and on your social networks. One simple strategy for increasing your list is to offer a monthly contest in which individuals subscribe to your mobile list to enter. You should also add a mobile opt-in field to your donate page and your e-newsletter subscribe page.

3. Add Your Text-to-Give Campaign to Your "More Ways to Give" Page

It's shocking how many nonprofits offer text giving, yet do not promote it on their website. Eighty-five percent of text donors have confirmed that small amounts donated via text does not decrease the overall amount they give to a nonprofit online or through direct mail,[9] so there's no need to fear that promoting your text-to-give campaign on your website will cannibalize other fundraising campaigns. Similar to mobile opt-in forms, you can also create a text donation opt-in form where donors can directly enter their mobile phone number on your website to receive the text donation confirmation text. In addition to a mobile opt-in form, your nonprofit should also include your keyword and short code on your website in case donors have their smartphones nearby and prefer to make the text donation directly rather than through an opt-in form.

4. Create Text-to-Give Graphics and Promotional Materials

To effectively promote your text-to-give (and text-to-subscribe) campaigns, you need to create images that include your keyword and short code that you can upload to social networks, especially as social networks become increasingly mobile and more visual. For example, if your text-to-give campaign is meant to raise money for wildlife conservation, then embed your keyword and short code on images of wildlife and then share the images on Facebook, Pinterest, Instagram, and so on. These graphics can also be added as sidebar images to your blog, used in email communications, and featured on your website. Additionally, and depending on your budget, purchasing TV ads, billboards, print media ads, or creating posters to promote your campaign in your local community has been proven to significantly increase text-to-give donations.

5. Promote Your Text-to-Give Campaigns on Social Networks

Social networks are a powerful driver of text-to-give donations, but not every day. Not even most days. When your nonprofit is responding to a crisis situation, breaking news, or current affairs, or when it's participating in cause awareness campaigns (such as World Water Day on March 22), those are the times to ramp up the promotion of your text-to-give campaigns to your social networks. Again, remember that text donors are impulsive and extremely responsive to text-to-give campaigns that foster a sense of urgency. Monitor what hashtags (a word or phrase pre-fixed with the # symbol) are going viral during these times on Facebook, Twitter, Google+, Instagram, and so on, and promote your campaign us-ing those hashtags. Then consistently tweet, share, and post interesting content intermingled with the promotion of your text-to-give campaign on the days when the crisis, story, or campaign is receiving a lot of media attention and buzz on social networks.

6. Promote Your Text-to-Give Campaigns at Fundraising and Cause Awareness Events

From marathons to galas, emcees should periodically inform attendees that they can make a donation via text. You could also include your key-word and short code in event materials. Activist organizations should promote their text-to-give campaign at protests and conferences. If your nonprofit has the connections, enlisting the help of musicians, actors, and athletes to promote your campaign at concerts, in interviews, and at sporting events has proven to be very effective in raising significant amounts of money.

7. Promote Your Text-to-Give Campaigns in the Evenings

Text donors give most often between the hours of 5 p.m. and 9 p.m. So your nonprofit should send text alerts asking for text donations in the late afternoon or very early evening. However, your nonprofit should be aware that some subscribers may be annoyed to receive mobile alerts during dinner or down time, so save your evening texts for the most im-portant fundraising pleas. Your donors and supporters are also very ac-tive on social networks on their smartphones in the evenings, often while they are watching TV, so your nonprofit should make a point to promote your text-to-give campaign on social networks in the evenings as well. When circumstances call for it, new media managers need to also work in the evenings.

8. Respond Rapidly to Breaking News

The person in charge of your mobile alert campaign should have a voracious appetite for breaking news and current affairs or your mobile alerts won't be timely. Your nonprofit must send your mobile alerts while the story is unfolding and going viral. Otherwise you will not be able to tap into the impulsive nature of text donors. The same is true for mobile alerts that are related to advocacy, such as texting mobile-optimized petitions or click-to-call appeals. If the story was headline news yesterday but no longer is today, odds are that you have already missed the opportunity to maximize your mobile alerts.

9. Emphasize the Year-End Giving Cycle

Since most giving occurs in December, your nonprofit should plan ahead and be prepared to send at least three mobile alerts in the month of December; one of these should be scheduled for one of the last three days of the year. Two of the three could focus on text to give while the third could ask for an online donation through your mobile-compatible donate page. Experiment and see which results in more funds raised. Similar to direct mail, many donors in December will perceive your mobile alert as a donation reminder. These donors often will not give using their smartphones, but instead will do so using your website on their PC or tablet.

10. Integrate Your Text-to-Give Campaign with Print Materials

In addition to online graphics, your nonprofit should create ads for your print newsletter for both your text-to-give and text-to-subscribe campaigns. You should also experiment with adding your text-to-give keyword and short code to print fundraising appeals, program brochures, and reports. Since text-to-give campaigns require a significant financial investment, you might as well use every communication channel at your disposal to maximize your text-to-give fundraising success.

MOBILE FUNDRAISING APPS

Odds are that by the time this book is published, a number of new mobile fundraising apps will be available that will tap into the power of using smartphones and tablets for fundraising. However, thus far the use of mobile fundraising apps by donors has not been widely adopted. This is largely because a mobile fundraising app with the potential for mass appeal has not yet been released. Over the last five years numerous fundraising companies have offered mobile fundraising apps to their nonprofit clients, but the majority of the apps have lacked in functionality and modern design aesthetics. In the early days of mobile fundraising apps, donate buttons linked to desktop donate pages, and the design of the nonprofit profiles inside the apps were reminiscent of late 1990s design aesthetics. For a mobile fundraising app to succeed, it has to offer an exceptional user experience, and thus far most mobile fundraising apps built by companies serving the nonprofit sector, though valiant in their attempts, have failed to deliver a mobile fundraising app that provides an experience compelling enough to detour donors away from direct mail or online giving.

However, with smartphones now outselling PCs in the United States and feature phones worldwide,[10] and tablets soon to follow, it's just a matter of time before new mobile fundraising apps are released that will finally meet a mobile donors' high expectations. For example, imagine the first mobile fundraising app that uses GuideStar as its database, thus enabling any nonprofit in the United States to create a nonprofit profile inside the app, but more importantly, allowing mobile donors to give to any nonprofit with simply a couple of taps inside the app. Donors could create profiles that save their credit (or debit) card information or are attached to their mobile wallet, thus eliminating the need for donors to enter their contact and credit card information with each donation. The donation history would be tracked in the app and transferable via email for tax reporting purposes. In addition, the perfect mobile fundraising app would include up-to-date information and news inputted by the nonprofit, calls to action such as tapping to sign petitions, the ability to create and promote mobile app-based social fundraising campaigns, and gaming strategies such as earning points and increasing rank for donating, fundraising, taking action, and sharing content from the app with social networks. Giving through-text could also be incorporated into such an app using text donation opt-in fields. The possibilities are limitless, though such an app would be extremely expensive to build, and this is probably why one does not yet exist. But it will. Mobile fundraising through mobile apps is an inevitable evolution in the mobile giving experience.

In fact, the first generation of this app does exist. Google's One Today App (google.com/onetoday) enables Android users to donate $1 a day to nonprofits that have signed up to create profiles on One Today. While the profiles are not generated from GuideStar, nonprofits that are members of the Google for Nonprofits Program (google.com/nonprofits) can participate in One Today. Donations are given and processed through Google's Mobile Wallet and then sent to the nonprofits through a partnership with Network for Good. In time, the app could offer additional calls to action, content publishing for nonprofits, gaming strategies, and of course integration with Google+. Clearly, it takes a company like Google with the financial resources and the technical infrastructure to build and launch such an app, but there's no doubt that more will follow. Your nonprofit would be wise to monitor this trend in giving very closely and embrace a strategy of early adoption.

In terms of social fundraising, mobile fundraising apps can help your fundraisers raise more money if the app is built to tap into the power of your fundraisers' social networks. Nonprofits that select a social fundraising software that is both mobile-compatible and offers a mobile fundraising app enable their fundraisers to raise up to three times more in funds than those nonprofits that do not.[11] Some of the large nonprofits that regularly launch event social fundraising campaigns, such as the American Heart Association, have built their own mobile fundraising apps to improve their success, but most nonprofits need not invest the financial resources to build their own app. Rather, they should simply promote the apps already created by the social fundraising or text-to-give software company that they have selected.

Finally, in the coming years we will see niche fundraising mobile apps become more successful and widely adopted. CharityMiles (charitymiles .org) is a mobile app that enables walkers and runners to donate with each mile they walk or run. There have also been numerous apps released that allow users to check in while shopping, earn points, and then convert the points into donations. However, most niche apps launched thus far have failed. Mobile fundraising through apps is challenging probably because only 16 percent of apps are opened more than twice after they are downloaded.[12] Mobile apps lose their appeal very quickly if they do not have a functionality and design that hooks users and keeps them tapping. Niche mobile fundraising apps still have a lot of potential, but the vast majority of those launched thus far haven't been successful. Perhaps the apps were a bit ahead of their time or mobile technology had not yet advanced enough for mass adoption, but all signs indicate that mobile fundraising apps of all kinds will play a significant role in the future in mobile and social fundraising. That said, early adopter nonprofits would be wise to follow the trend closely and experiment with new niche mobile fundraising apps, such as Check-in for Good (checkinforgood.com), I Can Go Without (icangowithout.com), and GiveMob (givemobapp.org) as well as any others that become available in the coming years.

MOBILE WALLETS

More than any other mobile payment processing technology, mobile wallets have the greatest potential for transforming fundraising, but the technology and its implications are not well understood in the nonprofit sector. Many incorrectly assume that mobile wallets are only for processing payments at retail establishments by scanning their smartphones, but mobile wallet services are increasingly offering digital wallet services that enable the ability to make payments online. Here's how the technology works: users download a mobile wallet app and then enter their credit card information inside of the app or through the wallet service's website. The credit card information is stored, and then users can scan and tap to pay at brick-and-mortar locations, or in the case of online payment processing, click or tap to add a payment to their wallet to thus have the payment automatically added to their credit card bill. This minor tweak in payment processing eliminates both the need to carry credit cards and the need to enter contact and credit card information when purchasing a product online or making an online donation. Since many mobile and online donors often give impulsively or are pressed for time, this simplification of the donation process could be transformational. In fact, mobile wallets could be the greatest advancement in mobile and online fundraising that the nonprofit sector has ever experienced.

Of all the mobile wallet services—V.me, Isis, PayPal, Lemon, and Dwolla—Google Wallet is the pioneer for online donation processing. It was the first, and as this book went to press, the only digital wallet service to offer donate buttons that nonprofits can add to their website and to their YouTube channel. In fact, in 2013 Google replaced Google Checkout with Google Wallet, and odds are that it will integrate Google Wallet with Google+ in the near future. Not be out done, Facebook is also rumored to be working on a mobile and digital wallet service, and Apple is actively building an IWallet app. And while PayPal-branded donate pages are not the best option for online donation processing, its mobile and digital wallet service could become widely used since the company already has more than 130 million active registered users.[13] In the near future, it is very likely that your donate page will not ask donors to choose which credit card they want to donate with, but rather, which wallet service.

Thus, it's also likely that in the future many of the current companies that offer online and social fundraising and crowdfunding software, like Network for Good, Razoo, and Indiegogo, will partner with mobile wallet services. It's also possible that future text-to-give campaigns will be empowered by mobile wallets rather than mobile carriers. Currently, a service called TapFunder (tapfunder.com) allows users to text a keyword and short code to receive a link to a mobile-compatible donate page where donors can enter contact and credit card information to make a donation rather than have the donation added to their mobile phone bill.

Imagine if instead donors were sent a link to a mobile-compatible donate page that featured an "Add to Wallet" donate button where all that was required on the part of the donor to complete the donation was one tap to add the donation, a tapped entry of their wallet password, and a second tap to confirm the donation. Take that even further and imagine a mobile alert sent by a nonprofit in a time of crisis that links to a mobile-compatible donate page where donors can tap to add a donation to their wallet. Once a nonprofit begins to imagine and conceptualize how mobile and digital wallets can be used to streamline mobile and online fundraising processes, the next step is experimentation and early adoption. As always, the early adopters tend to have the highest fundraising success. However, mobile wallets have yet to be widely adopted by consumers and donors, but one in three Americans now say that they would prefer to leave their purse or wallet at home when they go out shopping or for entertainment and instead bring their smartphone for payment processing if more brick-and-mortar businesses offered the capability to do so.[14] When you combine this trend with soaring smartphone sales and the ease of mobile and digital payments and donations, it's clear that the days of plastic credit cards, checks, and cash will soon be behind us and relegated to history.

NONPROFITS TO STUDY AND LEARN FROM

❑ National Wildlife Federation: nwf.org

❑ Humane Society of the United States: humanesociety.org

❑ Human Rights Campaign: hrc.org

❑ Greenpeace: greenpeace.org

❑ American Red Cross: redcross.org

2

CREATE AND MAINTAIN A MOBILE AND SOCIAL CONTENT STRATEGY

The success of your nonprofit's mobile and social fundraising strategy depends upon having a good mobile and social content strategy in place. The first part of this book focuses on helping your nonprofit make wise decisions about nonprofit technology in order to ensure that you have a solid foundation upon which to implement your content strategy. The two are entirely interdependent; if one is lacking, then the other will be hindered in producing success. But when your fundraising and content strategies work together, your brand recognition increases and your reputation as a nonprofit that achieves its mission and programs and creates lasting change for the better of society is solidified.

Understanding the importance of creating and distributing content to tell your nonprofit's story and inspire action is the basis upon which your content strategy is built. It requires a staff investment as well as good writing, editing, and photo and video editing skills—on both PCs and mobile devices. Until recently, media outlets were the sole creators of online content, but nonprofits are now learning that they also need to be reporters for their nonprofit and their cause(s). In the old days (circa 2005), the content strategy of most nonprofits consisted of publishing a website, an e-newsletter, a quarterly print newsletter, fundraising appeals, and an annual report. Until recently, this was enough. But with the proliferation of mobile and social media, content is becoming more complex and varied in its format. Infographics, 15-second Instagram videos, and branded photos—these are types of content that garner the highest interaction and engagement rates online.

This doesn't mean that the more traditional content commonly created by nonprofits is no longer valuable, but its format likely needs an upgrade to be compatible with today's online donors and supporters. There's a seismic shift occurring across all media that's changing longstanding design best practices as well as the life span of content. For most nonprofits this is uncharted territory. Regardless of your organization's size or capacity, outlining the type of content that your nonprofit wants to create and scheduling how that content will be distributed and on what channels is an essential first step for understanding the complexity of today's online communications and fundraising.

7

Multichannel Communications and Fundraising

The combination of nonprofit multichannel communications and fundraising is the use of multiple content distribution channels and fundraising tools that are integrated to complement and cross-promote each another. Central to the success of multichannel communications and fundraising is the ability of your nonprofit to create a wide variety of content ranging from print materials to online news stories, blogs, photos, videos, and reports. If your nonprofit is not creating content on a regular basis, then your mobile and social fundraising strategy will be severely hampered. A print newsletter, website, e-newsletter, and a donate page aren't enough to successfully engage and inspire five generations (gen Yers, millennials, gen Xers, baby boomers, and the silent generation) of donors and supporters. This is, quite simply, the reality of twenty-first-century communications and fundraising. Those nonprofits that focus on creating content and use as many communication channels and fundraising tools as their budget allows are the most successful in achieving their fundraising goals.

Central to the effective implementation of multichannel communications and fundraising is your nonprofit's brand. Your supporters and donors are much more likely to take your content seriously if your brand is both visually compelling and intellectually stimulating. At the core of your brand are your nonprofit's logo, avatar, and design scheme. All communication channels should be professionally designed, and it's important to understand that content should be created and distributed in a way that further uplifts your brand. When your nonprofit's brand is strong and effectively merged with your fundraising and content strategies, your nonprofit will begin to experience a synergy that manifests itself in very tangible ways, such as increased awareness of your nonprofit and the causes you advocate, increased website and blog traffic, increased email and mobile subscribers, rapid social network community growth, and therefore as a consequence, increased donations and event attendance.

Nonprofit communications and fundraising are much more complicated and time consuming than they were just five years ago. You begin first with a strategy built upon making wise technology and design decisions about your core tools—your database, print materials, website, email, and fundraising systems. Overlapping this strategy is your nonprofit's brand recognition and reputation. And then integrated with both are your content strategy and your ability to create and distribute content. Today's communications and fundraising are not easy, nor are they intuitive to most nonprofit communications and fundraising staff. But they are powerful when implemented, and the skills required to be exceptional in both your on and offline communications and fundraising campaigns can be learned and mastered.

WRITE A MOBILE AND
SOCIAL CONTENT STRATEGY

Not all nonprofits that excel at mobile and social media write out their content strategies. Many new media managers operate on a day-to-day basis, letting their intuition, creativity, and analysis of daily engagement metrics, such as shares, likes, retweets, repins, and +1's, dictate the next day's content strategy. It's an admirable skill, but a rare one. Most non-profits need structure and a schedule for creating and distributing mobile and social content to make their jobs manageable and less overwhelming. The unfortunate reality is that most new media managers also serve as communications directors, development directors, event planners, and perhaps even office managers as well. A full-time new media manager position is a rarity at most nonprofits. However, regardless of your nonprofit's capacity, similar to creating and implementing your mobile and social fundraising plan, you can also create and maintain a mobile and social content strategy that is workable and that moves your nonprofit forward.

Your content strategy is the process of planning and executing content creation and then distributing that content to maximize brand awareness and increase marketing metrics, engagement, and fundraising results. Similar to your fundraising plan, it must be flexible. Staff and volunteer hours fluctuate throughout the year, and new social networks are launched that need to be focused on, or not, depending upon your capacity. On the flip side, if some communication channels perform poorly, then a decision can made to drop the channel and replace it with another.

Writing your fundraising plan is your first priority. Once it's completed, your content strategy and editorial calendar should be written, added as an addendum to your fundraising plan, and implemented immediately. When crafting your content strategy, focus on these four questions:

- What cause(s) and issue(s) does our nonprofit want to be known for?

- How can our nonprofit assume leadership and become perceived as an expert source related to the cause(s) and issue(s)?

- Who are our key supporters and donors, and what are their preferred communication channels for getting information from our nonprofit?

- How will we track and report success?

The answers to these questions will affect where you focus in creating content and what tone and format your content should have, as well as what communication channels your nonprofit should be using to distribute your content. Part 1 of this book clarifies that your website, email communications, and online fundraising channels are the foundation upon which all other communication and fundraising campaigns should be based. However, with the rise of mobile and social media, your content strategy has to move beyond the core channels in order to build your brand and expand your reach.

Document 1: Your Mobile and Social Content Strategy

Overview

This section should begin with a summary of one to two paragraphs stating which cause(s) and issue(s) your nonprofit will focus on in your content strategy. It should clarify the fact that by creating a wide variety of content that is intelligent, informational, visually compelling, and sometimes editorial, your nonprofit will propel itself to a place of leadership and expertise on a local, state, national, or international level—depending on your mission and programs.

Goals

The primary goal of your content strategy is to emphasize content creation so that your nonprofit then has content to share on mobile and social media. If the content matches the wants of your supporters and donors, then their engagement with your content will result in more Facebook fans, Twitter followers, Instagram followers, and so on for your nonprofit. This section should therefore list the types of content (news articles, blogs, infographics, etc.) that your nonprofit plans to create, the communication channels (Facebook, Twitter, Instagram, etc.) that your nonprofit plans on using within the next 12 months based on the same 12-month cycle as your fundraising plan, and a set of specific goals, such as:

- Increase Facebook fans by 30 percent

- Increase Twitter followers by 30 percent

- Double Pinterest followers

- Double Google+ followers

- Double Instagram followers

- Achieve 5,000 YouTube video views

Each goal should be based on the current numbers that your non-profit has on the first day that your success spreadsheet goes into effect and not be overly ambitious. You want to be able to achieve your goals in the first year. Only after that first year of tracking social network community growth can you really have a clear understanding of what your goals should be in the years that follow.

It's better to focus on content that you can realistically create on a regular basis and then decide to use only a small number of communication channels and manage them well, rather than trying to use many channels and manage them poorly, which will reflect poorly upon your brand and likely in the process overwhelm, overburden, and eventually burnout your staff.

Action Items
Mobile and social media offer a multitude of possibilities for creating new content and expanding your reach. However, if it isn't done well, it's likely to produce only minimal results. Mobile and social media have permeated and intermingled with every communication and fundraising channel that exists on the web today, and, as a result, your supporters and donors expect your mobile and social media campaigns to be top notch. Thus, when crafting your action items, be selective and narrow down your action items to only those that can be implemented with professional polish, such as:

- Design new branding for our social network communities.

- Host quarterly Google+ Hangouts.

- Create a minimum of two blog posts weekly.

- Create an infographic summarizing our program success for the year.

- Launch a presence on Pinterest.

- Hire a part-time or full-time new media manager.

At the end of this section, explain in one or two sentences why the action item was chosen and how it will help you achieve your content strategy goals.

Update Your Budget and Your System for Tracking Success

The communication channels and action items selected for your content strategy will have a direct impact upon your fundraising plan's budget. Hire a graphic designer to create a new avatar and branding for your social networks, such as custom background images and banners. The design for infographics can cost between $2,000 and $3,000. If you decide to hire a part- or full-time new media manager, you will find that staff time is the most costly expense associated with implementing a comprehensive fundraising plan and content strategy. Salaries of new media managers vary widely depending upon location. Small nonprofits with limited budgets will be more constrained than will those of large well-funded organizations, but new media managers have a much sought-after skill set, and their value will only increase over the course of time.

Your content strategy will also require that additional metrics be added to your success spreadsheet (as discussed in Chapter 2). Similar to tracking website and blog traffic and e-newsletter subscribers on a monthly basis, you'll also want to add new rows to the spreadsheet for tracking growth in Facebook fans, Twitter followers, Instagram followers, and so on. Over time what the spreadsheet will reveal is a direct correlation between a rise in the growth of your social networking communities and a rise in your website and blog traffic, e-newsletter and mobile alert subscribers, online and mobile donations, and so forth. When sharing your success spreadsheet with key staff, the growth of your social networking communities will become one of the most watched and valued metrics. In many ways, mobile and social media are a numbers game. The early growth period is always the slowest for small to medium-sized nonprofits. But if your content strategy is sound, the math will reveal itself in tangible, trackable ways over time.

Some nonprofits track engagement metrics, such as the number of retweets, repins, or shares they get on social networking sites. Doing this can be very time consuming unless you are using an analytics tool (as discussed in Chapter 16). One thing to keep in mind is that as a result of high retweet, repin, and share rates, your followers will grow, so the two sets of metrics are intertwined. If you are limited on time, tracking your social network community growth is enough.

CREATE AN EDITORIAL CALENDAR

A nonprofit's editorial calendar is an outline of your nonprofit's content, when it should be created and by whom, and how often it should be distributed through your various communication channels and by whom. In the process of creating an editorial calendar, most nonprofits will discover that they have more content for their mobile and social media campaigns than they might realize. Excerpts from your print newsletter and email fundraising appeals can be used as blog posts; online event invitations, volunteer recruitment pages, website articles, and press releases can be shared on social networks; and branded images, slideshows, and video can be integrated across all online communication channels.

In addition to listing the content types and communication channels outlined in the goals of your content strategy, it's imperative that you also list who is responsible for each and provide an estimate of the number of weekly or monthly hours required for content creation and channel management. The numbers do not have to be exact or tracked on a weekly basis. The purpose is not to monitor every hour of how a staff member's time is spent, but rather to get staff members invested and have their time be valued. By listing staff responsibilities, your editorial calendar communicates clearly that there is a direct correlation between the investment in staff hours and the successful implementation and maintenance of your content strategy.

You likely already have job descriptions and a structure in place for print, website, and email communications, so the greatest challenge will be in deciphering how much time is required to utilize mobile and social media effectively (see Chapter 6). For nonprofits that have a full- or even part-time new media manager, adding new types of content and communication channels is fairly easy. But for those nonprofits that cannot hire new media staff and have to share the responsibility among multiple staff, creating new content and adding new channels is going to require that job descriptions change and responsibilities shift.

Document 2: Your Editorial Calendar

Your editorial calendar is the second and final document of your content strategy and the last and final document of your mobile and social fundraising plan. Since all content now has a direct impact on your mobile and social fundraising success, your editorial calendar should include everything from print fundraising appeals to blog posts to your online store. If it can be distributed (on or offline), it needs a line item in your editorial calendar. This will help your nonprofit conceptualize all the content that you have to work with and get it scheduled for distribution and cross-promotion.

Your editorial calendar can be created using an Excel spreadsheet or Outlook or an online calendar system. It can also be created through a project management system included in your CRM. For print and web and email communications that are fairly regular, such as print newsletters, news articles, blog posts, annual reports, and e-newsletters, use an annual calendar based on the same schedule as your strategic plan and input the projected publication dates. For events like an annual gala, Google+ Hangout, or tweet chat, add the projected publication dates of both the print (if applicable) and digital versions of the event invitation.

If you plan on creating infographics or publishing a case study or ebook, again add the projected publication dates. If your content is published earlier or later than expected, change the projected publication dates to actual published dates. Doing so will help you better estimate the time required to create and then publish the content in the future when you revise your editorial calendar.

For mobile and social media, you should add to your editorial calendar a weekly schedule for posting status updates, tweets, branded photos, and the like. Frequency of posting is discussed in detail for each social network in Chapters 9 through 14. Note that it's important to not set a schedule that is too rigid. Breaking news and fundraising and awareness campaigns may require that your nonprofit be more active one week and selecting exact posting times doesn't allow for new media managers to trust their instincts about their online communities. Rather, your mobile and social media schedule should detail the minimum number of posts required on a weekly basis to each mobile and social media channel and merely suggest the day of the week it should be posted.

Finally, whether it is done through color coding or by inserting columns into an Excel spreadsheet, every content type should have associated with it the name of the staff person responsible and the estimated number of monthly or weekly hours required to both create and distribute the content. Again, the primary purpose of doing this is to clarify the responsibilities of staff members and validate their time investment. By organizing and scheduling your content strategy, the responsibility for its success becomes a team effort. Even if you only have one or two staff members responsible for content creation and distribution, your editorial calendar can be shared with other staff. Mobile and social media campaigns that have organizational buy-in are much more successful than those done in isolation. Since the success of your mobile and social fundraising plan is contingent upon the creation and maintenance of your content strategy, having a comprehensive editorial calendar that clearly indicates that an investment in staff resources is necessary helps your nonprofit move beyond the harmful mythology that mobile and social media are free.

FIVE COMMUNICATION STYLES FOR NONPROFITS

Your content strategy thus far has focused on what types of content your nonprofit plans to create and what channels it will use to distribute the content. The next step is to start thinking about the tone of voice of your content. The easiest way to craft your tone of voice is to base it upon the mission of your nonprofit. If your nonprofit focuses on human rights or poverty, for example, then your tone of voice should be serious, smart, and thought-provoking. If your nonprofit works to protect the environment or animals, then your tone of voice could be informational, resolute, and sometimes even humorous. If you are an arts and culture organization, think about crafting a tone of voice that is creative, clever, and entertaining. Ask yourself: what are five words that describe the character traits of your mission or organizational culture? And then use these words to craft your tone of voice.

Your tone of voice should then become the basis for all. When writing and designing content, keep those five words at the forefront of your mind and work toward having those five words become synonymous with your online brand. Branding isn't only visual. It's also intellectual. Your tone of voice and your brand will then guide you as you actively employ the five communication methods most commonly used in the nonprofit sector. Storytelling should be your top priority, but it should be balanced with a steady intermingling of marketing, fundraising, engagement, and curation.

1. Storytelling

Communicating the stories of your nonprofit is the most powerful means of inspiring your donors and supporters. When done well, storytelling will evoke emotions ranging from empathy to anger that will galvanize your donors and supporters to take action on behalf of your nonprofit. In fact, 56 percent of individuals who follow nonprofits on mobile and social networks take further action, the number one action being making a donation, after they have read a compelling story published by a nonprofit.[1] Telling a good story requires a creative mind, excellent writing skills, and the ability to edit and brand images.

2. Marketing

Marketing is the strategic use of content and communication channels for direct gain. In the business sector, it's about selling products and services. In the nonprofit sector it's about securing more donors, e-newsletter subscribers, event attendees, and so on. Many nonprofits new to mobile and social media make marketing a high priority in their content strategy by repetitively asking for donors, e-newsletter subscribers, and event attendees. However, without storytelling, a heavily focused marketing approach is doomed to fail. Marketing on mobile and social media in the nonprofit sector needs to be subtle because most donors and supporters don't like being marketed to. Direct asks and calls to action are powerful online, but only in moderation and when balanced with storytelling.

3. Fundraising

Fundraising content embraces both storytelling and the concept of marketing, but it is unique in that its primary purpose is to inspire individuals and businesses to give money. A good story published on a blog that receives a lot of traffic *and* has a strategically placed donate button may result in a small number of passive donations, but fundraising content is written to tap into the core characteristics of what motivates donors to give online (as discussed in Chapter 5) and not just once but multiple times.

4. Engagement

For many years the dominant benchmark for whether a nonprofit is successfully using mobile and social media has been if it engages or not, but engagement for the sake of engagement is a flawed communication method. The overtouting of conversation as the ultimate metric of mobile and social media success has unfortunately been overdone. For example, many nonprofits mass thank their Twitter followers for retweets and their Facebook fans for every comment posted on their Facebook Page. This is both ineffective and a poor investment of time. To engage effectively is to respond genuinely to questions and comments and facilitate the discussions that your followers are having with each other. When more than 2,000 individuals who support nonprofits on social networks were asked what inspired them to donate money or items, or become a volunteer or attend an event, not one of them replied that it was because a nonprofit engaged with them on a social network.[2]

5. Curation

For nonprofits that cannot create content on a regular basis, embracing content curation can help you fill in the gap in your content strategy. On mobile and social media, whoever shares, posts, tweets, and features the best content wins. If you can't hire a designer to create an infographic but a nonprofit similar to yours in mission can, then retweet, repin, and share the infographic. It's the same with video, branded images, case studies, and so forth. Your donors and supporters follow you on mobile and social media first and foremost because they are connected to your mission and the cause(s) you stand for. Through content curation, there is a never-ending reservoir of top-notch content you can use to communicate your cause, uplift your brand, and inspire your donors and supporters.

FIVE CONTENT APPROACHES
THAT INSPIRE ACTION

From print to email communications, but especially on mobile and social media, there are content approaches guaranteed to inspire a reaction from your donors and supporters. Such approaches should be given high priority in your content strategy. Mastering the art of telling a success story, creating a sense of urgency, tapping into the power of statistics and quotes, and using a sense of humor take time to perfect, but once mastered, have a transformational effect on your online communications and fundraising campaigns. By consistently applying these approaches in your content strategy, little actions (a retweet) become bigger actions (signing an online petition) that become larger actions (making a donation). And when many little, big, and large actions reach critical mass, you have synergy and fundraising success at your fingertips.

1. Success

Donors and supporters want to read, see, and hear about the progress you are making in achieving your mission and programs. Increasingly results-driven, donors want to know that their donations are producing tangible results. Consistently giving donors and supporters progress reports is crucial to maintaining their commitment to your organization. Even if your nonprofit works on depressing issues such as war or domestic violence and there is little progress to be reported, there are always stories within your community that can be framed to showcase success. Positivity always trumps negativity across all social networks. Your donors and supporters like, retweet, +1, and repin positive stories over negative or depressing news stories on a ratio of five to one.[3] People hear enough depressing news from mainstream media. They don't want it from nonprofits.

2. Urgency

Creating a sense of urgency is a long-utilized practice in online communications and fundraising. When donors or supporters know that there is a deadline fast approaching and a limited time frame within which they can take action, they are much more likely to take action. This is why donors give generously during times of crisis. The funds are needed *now*, not next month or next year. Whether it's fundraising or advocacy, nonprofits that can frame stories that tap into the human impulse to take action in times of crisis have high success rates in their fundraising campaigns. Creating a sense of urgency also works well on mobile and social media. After positivity, the content with the greatest chance of going viral on social networks is the content that taps into breaking news and current affairs.

3. Statistics

Incorporating the use of statistics into your annual content strategy is a must. Each year create a page on your website or blog that lists 10 or more powerful stats that communicate the importance of your cause(s). Then throughout the year post one stat once a week on your social networks with a link to the stats page. Not only will these become your most retweeted tweets and shared status updates, but the page itself will become one of your most visited pages. It's counter to the idea that positivity is what gets attention, but powerful, shocking, and sometimes frightening stats often inspire an instantaneous reaction in your donors and supporters to take action. Your donors and supporters can easily digest 10 to 20 words, but may not take the time to read your 500-word blog post. Also, if your nonprofit has photo-editing skills, embedding the stats on images and then uploading them to Facebook, Twitter, Pinterest, and so on works even better.

4. Quotes

A quick Google or Bing search reveals a great number of inspirational quotes on a wide variety of causes that your nonprofit can use to its benefit. For mobile and social media, posting those quotes as text or as images (see Chapter 8) always garners a reaction and stimulates interaction and engagement. It's a tried-and-true tactic, and some would say a tired-and-true tactic. However, as long as quotes aren't overused to the point where your followers realize it is a tactic, nonprofits should embrace using inspirational quotes at least once a week in their content strategy. For fundraising content, quotes from donors or communities served are powerful. In addition, if your nonprofit has well-spoken executive or program staff, building your nonprofit's brand by quoting their wisdom and wit is a smart use of quotes.

5. Humor

The most challenging of all approaches, and not always appropriate, is the effective use of humor, which can increase online action and engagement. Being humorous online is a rare skill that requires creativity and a good dose of sarcasm. When done wrong, humor can be controversial or at the very least found to be in bad taste. But when done right, humor can become wildly popular. Humor is also the foundation of the phenomenon of *Kawaii*, a Japanese word meaning "cute." Scientifically proven to narrow focus and trigger positive emotions and reactions,[4] an explosion of nonprofits advocating for a wide variety of causes now find themselves tweeting, pinning, sharing, and blogging cute photos of baby animals and almost always with exceptional results. The act of uploading the files themselves is even beneficial in that viewing baby animal photos has also been proven to make workers more productive. *Kawaii* is powerful. Indeed, as the science of mobile and social media is starting to reveal, expanding your ideas about what is appropriate content is required.

10 NEWS ARTICLE AND
BLOG CONTENT IDEAS

Nonprofits are familiar with writing news articles and blog posts that provide program updates, tell success stories, comment on breaking news and current affairs, and promote calls to action. These types of news article and blog content are standard in nonprofit communications and should continue to be reported on regularly; however, some of your most shared, retweeted, and +1ed news articles and blog posts will be those that are out of the ordinary. With more than 250 million blogs in existence[5] and countless online news outlets worldwide, your new media manager must excel at writing and have the ability to expand his or her storytelling, marketing, and fundraising content beyond traditional news and blog writing. The rise of mobile and social media has profoundly altered how journalists frame and format their stories, and the same is true for nonprofit writers and bloggers.

1. Write Numbered Lists

Formatting your nonprofit's cause(s) and programs into numbered lists is guaranteed to grab the attention of your donors and supporters. Since most readers now scan online content rather than read it thoroughly, listing and bolding content in a numbered format ensures easy reading and piques curiosity. Examples of numbered lists include, "Five Reasons Why Conserving Wildlife is Important," "Ten Simple Ways to Serve Your Local Community," "Nine Powerful Stats about Domestic Violence in America," and "Six Reasons Why You Should Read to Your Children." Numbered lists have broad appeal on mobile and social media and are often read by individuals who have never been exposed to your nonprofit.

2. Photo Essays

Since most online readers scan content rather than consume it in its entirety, photo essays have emerged in recent years as a powerful means for telling a story. Your photo essay should include at least five images, and each image should fill the entire width of the page. Photos should include large bolded captions that explain what's happening in the photo. Additionally, all photos should be the same size and include a border. You should also preface your photo essay with one or two descriptive paragraphs and close your essay with a call to action.

3. Summarize Research Reports and Studies

Making a habit of summarizing the key findings of recently released research reports or studies is good strategy. Quite often the nonprofits or think tanks that release the report will promote your article or blog post. Since most reports and studies are released in association with a hashtag, you can promote your summary and gain access to new readers by using the hashtag on social networks. When summarizing a report, be sure to bullet-point at least five of the most important stats mentioned in the report. Then when distributing your summary, tweet or post one of the stats with a link to your summary. By including at least five stats in your summary, you can then distribute your summary up to five times over a one- or two-week period.

4. Share Resources Relevant to Your Cause

The Internet is a vast repository of resources. A simple search will reveal countless articles related to health, lifestyle, family, and popular culture. In addition, after breaking news and current affairs, it's the articles related to daily life that are the most popular on mobile and social media. Creative new media managers will expand their ideas about what their nonprofit can write about and experiment with publishing articles and blog posts that share resources and useful advice. For example, a health organization could write an article about the benefits of people consuming less salt. An environmental organization could write about which commonly bought food packaging items can be recycled. An organization whose mission is to support education could write a blog post about how parents can instill in their children at an early age the desire to go to college. Or an arts organization could write about the top 10 museums to visit in a lifetime. Very few nonprofits create this kind of content, but those that do have come to understand its power and integrate sharing resources into their long-term content strategy.

5. Show Donation Impact

Your nonprofit should regularly write articles and blog posts about how donations are being used and the impact they have had. For program milestones, illuminate how the funds that were raised helped you achieve the milestones. You should mention the amount raised and how many donors gave. In the process thank the donors and encourage others to give so your nonprofit can continue to move forward and achieve new milestones. You can also write about how your nonprofit decides which programs to assign a high priority and provide a timeline of the fundraising benchmarks that allowed your nonprofit to implement its programs. For example, if your nonprofit raised $10,000 to provide emergency supplies in the aftermath of a disaster, list all the products bought and delivered. Donors are much more likely to continue giving if there is concrete evidence that their donations are making an impact. You can also ask donors to submit statements about why they chose to give and integrate their quotes into your donation impact articles and blog posts.

6. Tell the Story of a Community Served

Evoking empathy is essential when telling the story of the communities or individuals that your nonprofit serves, or hopes to serve in the future. People who donate to nonprofits are empathic or they wouldn't give away their financial resources. They are motivated by simply knowing that they are making a difference or that they have the possibility to. Your challenge is to communicate the need through text, images, and video with dignity and respect for your communities, but in a way that also makes it clear that these communities and individuals are real human beings who are acutely affected by poverty, injustice, violence, or circumstances often out of their control. When telling their story, include quotes or video clips from community members and photos that do not objectify their need and wants, but rather illuminate how their needs and wants can be or are being met. Hope and possibility should be interwoven throughout the storyline. Otherwise donors will feel like the need is too great, and they may hesitate to give. A decade ago the storytelling of communities in need was meant to shock a donor into action. But with today's 24/7 news cycle that focuses on sensational and often depressing news, that style of storytelling no longer makes an impact in the nonprofit sector. Many donors have become numb to desperate pleas for help or feel overwhelmed and disempowered by them. Focusing on the positive that exists in even the most unfortunate of situations is much more likely to trigger a giving response.

7. Interview Donors and Volunteers

It's rare that a nonprofit interviews donors to give them the chance to share their thoughts and feelings about why they give. If you want to create a community of long-term givers who are more than just a collection of faceless database entries, then at least four times a year send a set of questions to donors willing to be interviewed, and ask them to include a photo of themselves that best represents who they are. Your donors will find it interesting to see the faces of other donors and read their stories and online supporters who have not yet donated may even be inspired to give. The same is true for volunteers. Potential volunteers want to read real stories based on actual volunteer experiences, not just marketing materials. For both donor and volunteer interviews, you can ask unique questions beyond the obvious to add more personality and character to the interviews, such as the next country they want to visit and why or how would they react if they won the lottery. In truth, for your content strategy to work, it has to expand beyond traditional news writing and blogging or your readers simply will not take much notice of your content, much less share it with their social networks.

8. Go Behind the Scenes

Many donors and supporters want to see what happens behind the scenes at your nonprofit. Take photos of important meetings and solicit quotes from staff about key takeaways from the meetings. Record a video of your office or facilities. You can also interview staff and volunteers as they are preparing for an event. Though donors are primarily concerned with the cause(s) you advocate, demonstrating how hard your staff works behind the scenes can further cement their commitment to your nonprofit.

9. Write Book and Movie Reviews

Writing reviews about popular books and movies whose plots and characters are related to the cause(s) your nonprofit advocates is an easy way to tap into pop culture. It's often perplexing when you read a book or attend a movie that evokes powerful emotions ranging from empathy to outrage, and the book's conclusion and the movie's closing credits rarely suggest how individuals can take action. It's a missed opportunity to foster social good and one that nonprofits can fill by occasionally writing reviews and commentaries on bestselling books and box office hits. Before distributing your reviews, search for popular hashtags representative of the book or movie.

10. Feature New Mobile and Social Media Content

When your nonprofit launches a new infographic, video, or ebook, for example, write an article or blog post that features the content. Often nonprofits will launch a new video, but simply link to their YouTube channel when distributing the video on social networks. This is a missed opportunity. By embedding the video into your website or blog and providing some background information on why and how the video was made, you'll likely get more video views and website traffic. The same is true for infographics. They should be featured on your website in proximity to a donate button, e-newsletter and mobile alert opt-in forms, and social network icons rather than being hosted on a third-party website. Infographics are very popular on mobile and social media, and converting infographic readers into donors, e-newsletter and mobile alert subscribers, and social network followers should be the dominant strategy behind creating an infographic. Also, if your nonprofit creates an ebook or online report, never directly link to a PDF version on social networks. Rather, create a summary on your website or blog about the ebook or report and then link to the PDF version in the website article or blog post. Even better, digitalize your ebook or online report directly inside your website. Finally, if your nonprofit launches a presence on a new social network, then write about your goals and ask your donors and supporters to help grow your new community.

8

Content Creation and Integration

The rapid rise of mobile and social media is having a profound impact on how your donors and supporters consume your content. Nonprofits need to reconsider the design and formatting of all of their content—from print materials to ebooks to event invitations—or risk not being able to stand out from the barrage of tweets, status updates, pins, text messages, and emails that donors and supporters now contend with on a daily basis. With millions of nonprofits, charities, and NGOs worldwide all vying for their attention, to stand out from the clutter, your communications and fundraising campaigns must be adapted quickly to new design aesthetics, and you must be willing to break with tradition and try something new. Today, it's unrealistic to expect donors and supporters to read heavily text-based content, and nonprofits must come to understand that most readers now skim text content and rely heavily upon images and video to digest your stories.

It's a given that all web-based content must now be mobile compatible, but your donors and supporters also expect social media integration into all of your content, even print. Social networks are popular all over the world and continue to grow. Odds are that your donors and supporters use them daily, if not at least weekly. Thus integrating your mobile and social media campaigns into all your content allows your donors and supports to easily find and support your nonprofit on social networks and consequently ensures that your social networks will continue to grow and become powerful channels for your content strategy.

PRINT MATERIALS

The print design best practices of newsletters, fundraising appeals, brochures, annual reports, and case studies have not evolved to reflect how individuals now consume content, and they desperately need to. The style of print materials that were being written and published a decade ago is still that of those arriving in mailboxes today. They are heavily text-based, photos tend to be small or nonexistent, and less than 5 percent of nonprofit print materials today make any mention of their social or mobile campaigns. With the majority of donations made in response to print materials being done online, donors will also want to follow you on social networks or download your new smartphone app provided that you let them know how to do so in your print materials. Nonprofits with lengthy print fundraising appeals may want to experiment with more postcard campaigns since it is becoming less likely that your donors actually read your print fundraising appeals.

Print Materials Checklist

❑ Increase the font size (to at least 13 points), and use less text.

❑ Use larger photos and more of them.

❑ Add the icons and URLs of your social networks.

❑ Create ads for your text-to-give campaigns and smartphone and tablet apps.

❑ Include video icons and shortened links to relevant videos.

NEWS ARTICLES AND PRESS RELEASES

The "News" section on nonprofit websites is most often the home of news articles and press releases. With 75 percent of journalists worldwide using social media to research their stories and 55 percent of them using social media to source their stories[1] (and most of them on mobile devices), it is clear that formats of news articles and press releases need to be entirely revised and used more strategically. Currently, most news articles embrace one-to-many communications (no social interaction), and press releases are still formatted in exactly the same way they were when distributing them to journalists required mail couriers and mass faxing.

News Article and Press Release Checklist

- ❏ Include social sharing and social commenting functionality.
- ❏ Always include a photo to increase the likelihood of social sharing.
- ❏ Ensure that e-newsletter and mobile alert opt-ins, social network icons, and a donate button are prominently featured.
- ❏ Include your nonprofit's Twitter username and relevant hashtags to your press release.
- ❏ Add links to relevant videos or downloadable high-res photos to your press release.

BLOGS

Blogging platforms were first launched in 1999 and marked the beginning of the rise of social media. Heavily adopted by nonprofits throughout the 2000s, blogging was the first type of content published to the web that enabled donors and supporters to comment publicly. Until then, all content was one-to-many and was heavily focused on marketing. Today, blogging is one of the most useful and easiest ways for nonprofits to create content. Nonprofits that blog have 55 percent more website traffic.[2] Unlike the early days of blogging when posts tended to be editorial and lengthy, blog posts today can be short in length and include only a slide show or a video and a sentence or two. The most commonly used CMSs—WordPress.org, Joomla, and Drupal—offer blogging platforms that can be hosted inside your website. But if your nonprofit cannot currently focus on launching a new responsively designed website, you can use WordPress.com, Blogger, or Typepad to launch a mobile-compatible blog that is separate from your website. At a later date when you upgrade to a new website and blog, you can transfer your old blog content to your new blog.

Blog Checklist

❏ Ensure that your blog is hosted inside your website to maximize your SEO.

❏ Ensure that e-newsletter and mobile alert opt-ins, social network icons, and a donate button are prominently featured.

❏ Always include a photo(s) to increase the likelihood of social sharing.

❏ Create sidebar graphics for special fundraising and advocacy campaigns.

❏ Embed videos inside your blog posts to increase video views on YouTube or Vimeo.

IMAGES AND INFOGRAPHICS

The use of branded images and infographics has become commonplace on mobile and social media and is a direct result of online users simply not digesting text as easily as they used to. Visual media is not a passing trend, and nonprofit communication and fundraising staff need some basic graphic design skills to stay current. Whether it's an advanced tool like Adobe Photoshop (adobe.com/photoshop) or a simple web-based photo-editing tool like PicMonkey (picmonkey.com), the ability to edit and crop images, embed text, and create banners and website and blog graphics is a must-have skill set for today's new media managers. If your nonprofit has a new media manager skilled enough to create custom infographics, consider yourself very fortunate. Most infographic design will have to be outsourced to skilled designers. There are, however, some simple, low-cost infographic design tools, such as Infogram (infogr.am) and Piktochart (piktochart.com), that your nonprofit can use to create visual images of your data and your program success.

If your nonprofit doesn't have a large library of images, Creative Commons (creativecommons.org) is an online database that offers royalty-free images, and Openclipart (openclipart.org) offers royalty-free graphics and clipart. Both sites are in compliance with copyright law. However, on occasion it is well worth purchasing high-quality and visually compelling stock photos and graphics from services like Shutterstock (shutterstock.com) and GraphicStock (www.graphicstock.com).

Images and Infographics Checklist

❑ Brand all images posted to mobile and social networks with your avatar and website URL.

❑ Create text-based images of powerful stats and inspirational quotes.

❑ Incorporate infographics into your print materials.

❑ Brand your infographics with your logo, tagline, and website URL.

❑ Use infographics as banners and backgrounds on social networks.

VIDEOS

Those nonprofits that can afford to invest in high-quality video equipment ($1,000 to $5,000) *and* have a talented and creative staff person who can dedicate time to creating and editing video, should rank video high in their content strategy. Often your donors and supporters will prefer to watch and listen to the success you are achieving in your mission and programs over reading about it. In fact, of those who support nonprofits on social networks, 41 percent have taken action (from donating money to becoming a volunteer) after becoming inspired by watching an online video posted on a social network.[3]

The problem is that most nonprofit videos are not professionally produced and thus have extremely low video views on YouTube and Vimeo. It's very difficult to create videos that people want to watch. Even if you can get your donors and supporters to press "Play," most will quit watching within the first 15 seconds if the video doesn't keep them engaged. Half of all Internet content may be video,[4] but that doesn't mean its good video. The truth is that for video to produce results, it has to be good. If you can afford it, it's often much easier and cost effective to hire an outside service. If you can't, focusing other kinds of content may be a better use of your time, or you can delve into creating microvideos using Instagram, Vine (vine.co), or YouTube Capture (youtube.com/capture) or use video collage tools such as Animoto (Animoto.com) and Qwiki (qwiki.com). All nonprofits should have at least one professionally produced video that summarizes its mission and programs and highlights its success. But to state that all nonprofits should be creating video on a regular basis is unrealistic.

Video Checklist

❏ Embed videos into your website and blog and share your videos on mobile and social media.

❏ Add call-to-action overlays to your videos with links to your website and social networks.

❏ Insert screenshots of videos into email communications that link to the video embedded on your website.

❏ Add video to social fundraising and crowdfunding campaigns.

❏ Add video to ebooks and digital reports.

ONLINE PETITIONS

For those nonprofits that engage in advocacy and online activism, the rise of online social networking has been a boon for increasing signatories and e-newsletter opt-in rates. Hundreds of millions of people worldwide have signed an online petition over the last decade, and petitions make great content for e-newsletters, call-to-action blog posts, social networks, and mobile alert campaigns. Some activists consider online petitions to be the epitome of "slackactivism," an online action that has little or no practical effect other than to make the person doing it take satisfaction in the feeling they have contributed.[5] Mainstream media have given a lot of coverage in recent years to online petitions that go viral and result in positive change. Small actions are better than no action at all, but it's true that online petitions with small numbers of signatories rarely create change. Nonetheless, online petitions are simple to create and worth adding to your content strategy if you are an advocacy or activist organization. Many comprehensive CRM systems offer online petition software, but your nonprofit can also explore using Change .org, Causes (causes.com), Care2 (care2.com), Avaaz.org, and TakePart (takepart.com). When selecting an online petition service, be sure that the petitions are mobile compatible and have modern design aesthetics.

Online Petition Checklist

❏ Limit text, increase font size, and use large visually powerful images or embed a video.

❏ Ensure that online petitions have social sharing functionality.

❏ Add social network and mobile alert icons and a donate button to your "Thank You for Taking Action" landing page and follow-up emails.

❏ Build your mobile action network by adding a mobile alert opt-in field to your petitions.

❏ If your petition concerns an elected official or a corporation, add a request to your petition and your thank-you email that requests that signatories leave messages of protest on the elected official or corporation's Facebook Page or mention them on Twitter.

ONLINE CONTESTS

Nonprofits can launch online contests to raise money, build their email or mobile lists, and increase cause awareness. The most successful contests offer prizes for those who make a small donation or submit their email address or mobile number in order to enter the contest. Also, the greater the prize, the more entrants you'll get. To build a compelling contest, solicit in-kind gifts for prizes, set a clear entry deadline, and build a visually compelling page on your website specifically for contest promotion and entry. You can also use services like Wildfire (wildfireapp.com) and ShortStack (shortstack.com) to host a contest directly on your Facebook Page. However, be aware that custom tabs on Facebook Pages are not visible on mobile devices and that there's the possibility that future Facebook Page designs will not include custom tabs. At the time this book went to press, the last Facebook Page design upgrade was the launch of the Timeline design in February 2012. Odds are a new design is in the works and is coming soon. Finally, 360 Photo Contest (360photocontest.com) is a unique service specifically for nonprofits. It merges social fundraising with voting. Entrants upload photos and then ask friends and family to vote for their photo by making a donation.

Online Contest Checklist

❑ Prominently feature e-newsletter or mobile alert opt-ins as the contest entry method.

❑ If fundraising is your goal, prominently feature a "Donate" button and clarify that online donors are entered in the contest twice.

❑ Ensure that your online contest page has social sharing functionality. Also be sure that your nonprofit's social network icons as well as those of your sponsors are prominently featured in order to increase the likelihood of sponsors promoting your contest.

❑ Create a hashtag for the contest and promotional graphics, and then promote your contest heavily on mobile and social media in the weeks leading up to the contest.

❑ Send follow-up "Thank you for Entering" emails that include your social network and mobile alert icons and a donate button and that have social sharing functionality.

ONLINE STORES

In the past creating an online store to sell T-shirts or bumper stickers was a costly, time-consuming endeavor that prevented most nonprofits from selling anything online. However, as mentioned in Chapter 5, a good online fundraising service will create a simple online store as part of its monthly fee or as a low-cost add on. For advanced online stores, Shopify (shopify.com) for as little as $29 a month for 100 products, will allow you to host on an online store inside your website that comes complete with payment processing, automatic shipping calculation, invoicing, and analytics. Once created, your online store and the product pages can be used as part of your content strategy. Shopify is mobile compatible, which is important when you consider that annual mobile commerce sales are expected to rise to $109 billion by 2017.[6] Additionally, there is Aradium (aradium.com), which enables nonprofits to host an online store directly inside their Facebook Page for as little as $15 a month.

Online Store Checklist

❑ Enable social sharing of your products, especially for Pinterest.

❑ Enable product reviews that can be shared on mobile and social networks.

❑ Add social network and mobile alert icons to your "Thank You for Purchasing" landing page and follow-up emails.

❑ Create graphics to promote your online store and special sales on your website on your blog, in your e-newsletter, and on mobile and social media.

❑ Send mobile alerts to feature products and special sales.

EBOOKS AND DIGITAL REPORTS

Print materials such as annual reports, case studies, and magazines can be easily converted into digital format at a very low cost. After a setup fee of $349 per publication and $5 per page, BlueToad (bluetoad.com) enables page flipping, smartphone and tablet compatibility, custom branding and tool bars, and multimedia integration. Your publications can then be submitted to the app stores and newsstands of Apple, Android, and Amazon. Rather than just converting your print materials to PDF and uploading them to your server, there are many new tools available to nonprofits that help them better feature their print content online and in the process save them thousands of dollars in print expenses. For nonprofits that publish lengthy print materials on a regular basis, 3D Issue (3dissue.com) is a software (starting at $1,300) that enables your nonprofit to create unlimited ebooks and digital magazines that are compatible with app stores and digital newsstands. Finally, for nonprofits with limited budgets that want to experiment with new ways of presenting their print content online, Urberflip (uberflip.com) allows nonprofits to create mobile-compatible, web-based digital reports that can include images, links, audio, video, and maps and that are shareable on social networks.

Ebooks and Digital Reports Checklist

❑ Increase font size and feature large images and call-to-action buttons.

❑ Ensure that e-newsletter and mobile alert opt-ins, social network icons, and a donate button are prominently featured.

❑ Embed YouTube or Vimeo videos and slideshows.

❑ Create graphics to promote your ebooks and digital reports on your website, on your blog, in your e-newsletter, and on mobile and social media.

❑ Link to your smartphone apps, if applicable.

EVENT INVITATIONS

In recent years fundraising event invitations and promotional materials have become increasingly digital. Purchasing tickets online, as well as issuing tickets and tracking ticket sales, has become much easier for both attendees and nonprofits. Most comprehensive CRM and online fundraising software offer event management software. However, your nonprofit can also use event invitation and management tools such as EventBrite (eventbrite.com), Tito (tito.io), and DoAttend (doattend .com), all of which are mobile compatible. Ticket processing fees average 3 percent for paid events, and most services do not charge to create event invitations for free events. Additionally, to promote your paid events, you can use Facebook Events and Google+ Events and link to your event payment processing page.

Event Invitations Checklist

❑ Add social sharing to all online event promotions, the invitation itself, and ticket confirmation emails so that your supporters can invite their friends to attend.

❑ Add an opt-in for mobile alerts so attendees can be texted event updates and reminders as well as a save-the-date message for your next event.

❑ Include the hashtag for the event in all online event promotions.

❑ If it is an annual event, add a video or slideshow from last year's event.

❑ Create graphics to promote your events on your website, on your blog, in your e-newsletter, and on mobile and social media.

WEBINARS

Offering free live webinars about your work and the cause(s) your nonprofit advocates can help you to position your nonprofit as a leader and significantly grow your email list. However, if you want to present webinars for audiences of between 101 and 1,000 attendees, webinar software is expensive ($500 a month). But through TechSoup.org's software donation program, qualified nonprofits can get a 50 percent discount for GoToWebinar (gotowebinar.com). Another well-known webinar software used by nonprofits is ReadyTalk (readytalk.com), but it currently does not offer discounts for nonprofits that want to present webinars for more than 25 attendees. All webinars can be recorded and then uploaded to your website or your YouTube channel for postwebinar promotion.

Additionally, you could use the screen sharing option in Google+ Hangouts On Air to present a webinar to a large audience for free, but attendees must be a member of Google+ to join your webinar. If your nonprofit would like to use webinars for remote staff or board meetings, Skype Premium allows you to host webinars for 10 people or less (skype.com/premium) for only $5 a month.

Webinars for large audiences have to be visually compelling and fast-paced in order to maintain the interest of attendees. The webinars must be promoted on all your online communication channels to ensure high registration rates. Nonprofits could host webinars for enlisting and training online activists, to announce new programs, and feature special guests. Note that free webinars have an average 50 percent attendee rate, and unless you have celebrity-like special guests, it would be very difficult to convert webinars into fundraisers by charging a webinar registration fee.

Webinar Checklist

❑ In you webinar presentaion, include links to your website and social networks. Visit the links live during the presentation and recommend that attendees follow you, download your mobile app, opt-in to mobile alerts, and so on.

❑ Ensure that a staff person is tweeting live during your webinar and include the hashtag for the webinar in all webinar promotions.

❑ Add your webinars to your online events calendar.

❑ Email a set of follow-up notes to all attendees and no-shows that prominently features social network icons, a donate button, and a mobile alert opt-in.

❑ Archive recorded webinars on your website, and ensure that e-newsletter and mobile alert opt-ins, social network icons, and a donate button are prominently featured.

SMARTPHONE AND TABLET APPS

The vast majority of nonprofits do not need to launch a smartphone or tablet app. The cost associated with building an app is too high for most nonprofits ($25,000 to $50,000). Even more important, unless your nonprofit has a mission and programs particularly relevant to smartphone and tablet users, then the app will likely not reach a critical mass in downloads making the app not worth the financial investment. Donors and supporters will not repeatedly open an app to simply read your nonprofit's news or blog feed or see your more recent Facebook updates and tweets. For a nonprofit to launch a successful app, the purpose of the app must fill a niche that is not already met by other apps on the market and that taps into the addictive impulse found in smartphone and tablet users. Gaming, news, and lifestyle apps are the most downloaded and continuously used apps. Thus unless your nonprofit publishes a magazine or books (The National Audubon Society Field Guides Apps), has a large activist network willing to sign petitions inside a mobile app (Peta Action Alerts App), or offers lifestyle tips (American Red Cross First Aid App), then you shouldn't add an app to your strategic plan and content strategy.

If your nonprofit does want to launch an app, it's critical that you launch both iOS and Android versions. You should also investigate the cost of launching a version for Windows Phone. The percentage of Windows Phone users is *currently* small in comparison to Apple and Android, but similar to how Apple products are built to sync with one another, so are the suite of new Windows products. You may even want to consider launching a Windows 8 (soon to be Windows 9) app version of your smartphone and tablet app since the Windows OS is now app based. In terms of charging users to download an app, the app stores take 30 percent of your revenue in transaction fees. Unless your app is excellent and the reviews say as much, it will be a challenge to break even. If your nonprofit is still convinced that you have a unique app to offer your donors and supporters and the funds necessary to hire top-notch programmers and graphic designers, the success of your app depends much upon how well you promote it.

Smartphone and Tablet Apps Checklist

❏ Create a page on your website exclusively for describing the functionality of your app and include screenshots, app store "Download" buttons, and a mobile alert opt-in and social network icons.

❏ Create graphics to promote your app on your website, on your blog, in your e-newsletter, and on mobile and social media.

❏ Send a mobile alert linking to the app promotion page on your website.

❏ Create full-page ads in your ebooks and digital reports to increase downloads.

❏ Use push notifications (pop-up messages that appear within apps) to increase the open rates of your app.

3

USING MOBILE AND SOCIAL NETWORKS TO DISTRIBUTE CONTENT

The Internet is at a tipping point. It's estimated that by late 2014 or early 2015 the majority of adults will get their information from social networks rather than search engines and that social networks will become the primary source of referral traffic to your website and blog.[1] Any doubts that social networks aren't powerful or don't need to be prioritized in your online communications and fundraising campaigns can now be put to rest. The sooner your nonprofit can master content distribution on social networks, the more likely (and faster) your fundraising and content strategies will result in success. Nonprofits have been experimenting with mobile and social networks for years. Sadly many of them do not fully understand how social networks are different from traditional online communications and fundraising, and consequently nonprofits are making many mistakes that are hampering their success.

The effective use of social networks is a skill not to be underestimated. Each mobile and social network has its own unique tool set and etiquette, and only the most observant new media managers have learned what makes each social network unique and then adapted that knowledge to their content strategy. There are universal best practices that can be applied to all social networks. To avoid being repetitive by listing these best practices in each of the chapters dedicated to social networks, those universal best practices are:

- **Prioritize storytelling over marketing.** The five content approaches of success, urgency, statistics, quotes, and humor should be interwoven throughout your social network strategy. Increasingly, donors and supporters follow causes on social networks. If you make storytelling a higher priority than marketing, then over time your nonprofit's brand becomes synonymous with the cause(s) you advocate. In practice, for every five status updates, posts, or tweets, four should be related to storytelling (through blogs, website articles, video, photos, stats, and quotes), while only one should be a direct ask such as a marketing or fundraising pitch. The only exception is in crisis situations where urgent calls to action require mobilizing your social networking communities to donate, volunteer, or participate in advocacy campaigns.

- **Visuals inspire higher interaction and engagement rates.** Photos uploaded to Facebook get five times the interaction and engagement rates than posted links. Visually compelling photos uploaded to Twitter double retweet rates. Links shared on Google+ are mostly ignored while photos garner high +1 rates and shares. And Pinterest and Instagram, two of the most popular new social networks, are entirely image- and video-based. This reflects a seismic shift away from text to visual content. If you want your nonprofit to be highly shared, retweeted, +1d, repinned, and liked, then you absolutely must have photo-editing skills and a digital image library to work with.

- **Engage authentically.** Your nonprofit is not a person. It is a brand representative of a cause(s), and most causes require a tone that is smart, well-informed, and communicated with conviction. Much of the popular social media advice in recent years is given by people whose expertise is based on building their own personal brand, not the brand of a nonprofit or business. They often advocate that brands prioritize chatting and thanking their followers and that brands respond to every single mention or comment. It's a strategy that works well for building a personal brand, but not for a nonprofit brand. Some informal engagement is required by nonprofits of course, but only in moderation. In most cases, the best practices of building a personal brand on social networks should not be applied to building a brand for your nonprofit. Building a strong personal brand requires "being human" on social networks, but building the brand of your nonprofit should focus more on becoming an expert resource and a compelling storyteller.

- **Do not automate content between social networks.** Just because you can automate content, doesn't mean you should. Facebook allows status updates to be automated to Twitter, but Twitterers find it annoying. Instagram allows your photos to be posted to Twitter, but photos uploaded directly to Twitter get much higher retweet rates. HootSuite enables you to post the same message to multiple social networks with one click, but your donors and supporters have no interest in following robots. Be very wary of miracle marketing automation tools. Mobile and social media require authenticity and a time investment to be effective.

- **Be a content curator.** From Facebook to Instagram, very few nonprofits create enough quality content to have an effective content strategy when utilizing multiple social networks. Regularly getting in the habit of searching, sourcing, and posting, thus curating, interesting content to your social networks is a must-have skill for your new media manager.

- **Tap into breaking news and current affairs.** Regardless of whether your nonprofit is local, national, or international, nonprofits need to be ready to respond to breaking news and current affairs. Some of your highest interaction and engagement rates will occur when you create and distribute content that is timely and relevant to news stories that are going viral.

- **All social networks are mobile.** When distributing content on social networks, you need to assume that the majority of your content is being viewed on a smartphone or tablet. Studying how your nonprofit's content is displayed on social networks on mobile devices will further illuminate how visuals often work best on both PCs and mobile devices, and thus highly impact your content strategy.

- **Content frequency is dependent upon capacity.** Many nonprofits want to know exactly how often they should post on each social network. There are data to give you reference points (discussed in the following chapters), but to post effectively requires thought and creativity, not just hitting a quota for the day. The ability to be both effective and active on social networks is directly related to how many staff hours your nonprofit allocates to mobile and social media (see Chapter 16). Conversely, nonprofits that have the capacity to be consistently active on social networks need to also understand that there are negative consequences to posting too often.

- **Professional graphic design is essential for effective branding.** Internet users have become highly advanced and now expect quality graphic design in all your online communications and fundraising campaigns. On social networks, they will make a snap judgment about your credibility based upon your branding. If your avatar, banners, and backgrounds are professionally designed, then users are much more likely to become followers. Whether they remain followers becomes dependent on how well your nonprofit understands and uses social networks.

9

Facebook

With more than 1 billion active users, Facebook is the largest social network in the world. Its users are also the most diverse in age, race, class, gender, and rural versus urban demographics and consequently the best online manifestation of society as a whole. More than two-thirds of Facebook users log in every day, and three-fourths of Facebook users do so on a mobile device.[1] Without a doubt your nonprofit's donors and supporters use Facebook on a regular basis. Therefore, Facebook should be your first priority and entry into social networking. However, to stand out from the other 50 million Facebook Pages regularly active within the Facebook community all vying for likes, comments, and shares, and to ensure news feed exposure, your nonprofit needs to excel at Facebook. Many nonprofits don't realize that exposure in the news feed is given only to those pages that consistently get high interaction and engagement rates. Without news feed exposure, there's little point to being active on Facebook.

The year 2014 marks the tenth anniversary of Facebook's launch. Over the last decade the Facebook Page tool set has evolved many times, and best practices have become more advanced. Facebook is a great tool for building your online brand, fostering community around your cause(s), and increasing referral traffic, but understand that without making investments in graphic design, good content creation, and possibly advertising, your Facebook strategy can go only so far. It's powerful, but not miraculous. Too many nonprofits have a myopic view of Facebook which manifests itself in posting too often or neglecting other social networks. Even the smallest of nonprofits should be active on at least two social networks for the sake of diversifying their brand and to become a more skilled, well-rounded social networker.

FACEBOOK FOR FUNDRAISING AND CAUSE AWARENESS

Facebook's greatest strength is its ability to enable your nonprofit to tell your stories on a regular basis to donors and supporters. Although it's difficult to prove in monetary amounts, it has been proven that 59 percent of fans will eventually make an online donation to the nonprofits and causes they care about if they are inspired by a nonprofit's storytelling on Facebook.[2] While your direct fundraising asks may be met with silence on Facebook if they lack creativity, fans do mentally note over time your nonprofit's progress in achieving its mission and programs through the status updates you post. Increasingly, the process of storytelling through status updates is converting fans into donors, volunteers, and event attendees.

Even more telling is that the primary reason that individuals follow your nonprofit on Facebook is that it publicly displays their support of your nonprofit to their friends and family in the news feed through their own personal status updates, shares, and likes.[3] In and of themselves, engagement and interaction have become activist activities on Facebook. Some may discount this as being slackactivism, but that undervalues the growing trend that fans evolve and become more dedicated to your nonprofit and your cause over time on Facebook. Half of the individuals who follow nonprofits on Facebook follow only five nonprofits total.[4] Therefore, if they have followed your page and continue to follow your page over months or years, then your responsibility is to keep them inspired and engaged because at some point more than half of them will donate to your nonprofit. Furthermore, some of your fans will also tap into their Facebook friendships to fundraise for your nonprofit and this friend-to-friend activity is definitely resulting in real dollars raised in social fundraising campaigns. Fifteen to eighteen percent of all social fundraising campaign donations are now referred directly from Facebook.[5]

TOP FIVE FACEBOOK PAGE
BEST PRACTICES FOR NONPROFITS

The Facebook Page tool set appears very straightforward. Quite simply, you post a status update, it gets published to the news feed (maybe), and then as the administrator (admin) of your page, you monitor your status updates for comments, likes, and shares. Then you respond accordingly. However, a deeper look into status updates and the admin panel reveals a much more advanced tool set with hidden features that unfortunately the vast majority of nonprofits never experiment with or use to their advantage because they do not take the time to explore the tool set thoroughly. Too often nonprofit admins of Facebook Pages become so entrenched in their Facebook habits that they don't even realize that there have been upgrades to the tool set. Being fluid in your approach to all social networks and remaining open to change and learning is crucial to success.

1. Know Well the Functionality of Status Updates

Ninety percent of the power of your Facebook strategy rests on the status updates. How you post your content has the greatest impact on whether your status updates will be shared, liked, or commented on and consequently whether your nonprofit will get consistent exposure in the news feed. Facebook applies a mysterious score based on an algorithm to your Facebook Page that dictates what percentage of your fans see your status updates in their news feed. No one knows exactly what the baseline score is (guestimates range from 5 to 10 percent), but you can ensure that your page scores on the high end by knowing well the functionality of status updates.

For example, uploading a visually compelling photo and then posting a status update with a short message and a link to your website or
blog is more likely to get interaction and engagement than just posting
a message and automated link and image, thus improving your score.
However, if you only post status updates in this manner, the strategy becomes less powerful because Facebook then lowers your score for only
uploading photos. A balance between uploading photos with a message
and link and posting status updates that include a message and automated link and image is the best practice. Out of every five status updates, it's recommended that three to four be uploaded images with a
message and link.

Posting links, however, isn't as straightforward as it appears. When
you enter a message and a link in the body of the status update, an automated link and image will automatically attach to your status update.
What many nonprofits don't realize is that you can then edit the link title and summary to make them more eye-catching by simply hovering
over and clicking on the link title and summary. You can also upload a
new image if the one automatically generated isn't visually compelling
enough to grab the attention of your fans in their news feed.

Also, by taking a closer look at status updates *literally*, you'll discover that there is also a scheduling function; the ability to target your
status updates by age, gender, location, education level, and language;
and the functionality to tag pages that have Facebook Location added to
their pages. You can also create milestones, highlight status updates, and
use hashtags. The icons and drop-down menus for these functions have
been in front of the eyes of millions of nonprofit admins every time they
post to Facebook, but until they're pointed out, many admins don't realize these functions exist.

Finally, never simply post a link to Facebook without attaching a
short message. That's Facebook marketing at its worst and does not inspire interaction and engagement thereby guaranteeing that your nonprofit's score will be very low. Whether it's an uploaded photo, a video,
or a link with an automated image, all content must be accompanied with
a short message written in your nonprofit's unique tone. Also, occasionally craft your message in the form of a question. Questions are a proven

tactic to increase comments, but they result in the fewest likes and shares so use them only occasionally to add variety to your page. Shares are the most powerful form of interaction on Facebook, and increasing your share rate should be a priority. Not surprisingly, visually compelling photos get the highest share rate of all content posted to Facebook. Once your nonprofit begins to experience high share rates—and the surge in new fans that result in the days after—posting shareable content will likely move to the top of your Facebook strategy.

2. Regularly Browse Your Admin Panel for Upgrades

Facebook is constantly tinkering with the Facebook Page tool set. Unless you make a habit of browsing your admin panel on a regular basis, your nonprofit could be missing out on powerful new upgrades. Some of your best learning occurs when you just start clicking around and experimenting with unused functionalities. It is obvious when you see a nonprofit Facebook Page that doesn't have a username, doesn't get recommended when others like similar pages, or doesn't have featured pages that the admin has not taken the time to thoroughly explore the admin panel.

3. Study Your Facebook Insights

Facebook Insights provide excellent data about your fans and their engagement and interaction with your page. Using Insights regularly to guide your Facebook strategy will help your admin get a very clear sense of what kind of content your fans respond to, which content they share, what time they are online, and where they are located, their gender, their age, and even what language they primarily communicate in on Facebook. If a post receives an extraordinarily high "Reach" (the number of people who have your content posted in their news feed), then you know to post more of the same kind of content. If your fan count spikes or plummets in one particular week, examine what kind of content you posted that week. Study carefully where your new fans come from as well. Most often they are the result of activity inside the Facebook community, rather than from external sites. You may also be surprised to discover that you have a large number of fans based in cities outside of your time zone, and thus you must post at different times to reach all of your fans. For being a free service, Facebook provides a very comprehensive set of analytics that can be used to guide you to becoming an excellent admin for your nonprofit's page.

4. Optimize Your Page for Facebook Graph Search

Unlike search engine results, which are primarily based on keywords and page titles, Facebook Graph Search allows users to search for pages based on keywords or themes, and the search results are highly affected by the liking activity of their friends. For example, searching for "animal shelters St. Louis, Missouri" will result first in those animal shelter pages liked by your friends on Facebook, rather than just a long list of pages with the words "Animal Shelter + St. Louis + Missouri" in their Facebook Page title. This can be especially powerful for small and medium-sized nonprofits that are regional since the majority of friends are also located in the same town or state. For nonprofits that are national or international, if you search "human rights" for example, the first pages listed (after those you like already) will be those human rights organizations liked by your friends. Since friend-to-friend activity and recommendations are powerful inside the Facebook community, nonprofits have much to gain from Facebook Graph Search.

To optimize your page for Facebook Graph Search, be sure to fill out your entire profile (about, mission, description, awards, topics), add your address, and enable your page to be tagged in photos. Facebook Graph Search places a strong emphasis on photo search results. Thus the more often your page is tagged in photos, the more exposure your nonprofit will receive in search results. This also means that your nonprofit should develop the habit of tagging your own photos. For example, if you are an animal shelter, tag your photos "Animals," and thus your photos are added to the search result "Photos of Animals."

5. Post Four to Six Times Weekly

How often your nonprofit should post on Facebook varies widely depending upon the size of your community and the type of content you post. However, it's important to know that the number one reason your donors and supporters unfollow your page is that they think you post too often.[6] One of the most valuable skills in a qualified admin is knowing that thin line between posting too many status updates and annoying your fans or posting just the right number that keeps them engaged and retained as a fan.

Large nonprofits with more than 100,000 fans that have good content and brand recognition can post up to two times a day. The fans they lose by posting that often are made up by the volume of shares they receive that then consequently results in new fans. Small and medium-sized nonprofits don't have the number of fans necessary to ensure high share rates and thus are more likely to lose as many or more fans than they gain from posting twice daily. Consequently, their fan count stagnates or grows very slowly. Additionally, your first post of the day has the highest score, and with each post thereafter your score drops significantly. Facebook does not want tens of millions of pages cluttering the news feed with multiple daily status updates, so Facebook systematically drops your score the more you post throughout the day. Insights, when examined carefully, will reveal this to be true. In fact, quite often your score will be higher across all posts if you post only every other day. In general, and though it may be difficult to curb your daily Facebook habit, posting four to six times weekly tends to result in the highest fan growth and retention rates, especially if you are a small- to medium-sized nonprofit.

Scientific data that analyzed the posting frequency of 1.1 million Facebook Pages confirmed that posting less often is a smart strategy. In fact, the data suggested that posting only four times a week is the optimal amount, as well as posting at noon for optimal shares (when people are on their lunch breaks) and on Saturday mornings (when people are enjoying Facebook, rather than working it).[7] While this frequency of posting recommendation goes against the vast majority of Facebook advice given in the blogosphere, a quick glance at your unlike rate as well as reach clearly shows the strongest result is when you post only four to six times a week.

FACEBOOK GROUPS

Before Facebook Pages were launched in 2007, Facebook Groups were the powerhouse of online community outreach for nonprofits. The early adopter nonprofits used groups to organize large communities around causes and issues. However, with the rise of Facebook Pages, Facebook began to scale back the functionality of groups to the point that by 2009 most groups were abandoned by their nonprofit admins as they shifted their priorities to their Facebook Page communities. Facebook then officially launched a new group design and functionality in 2010. While the new groups have never become as popular as the old groups, the new groups are very useful for helping nonprofits organize small groups of individuals such as volunteers, staff, and activists.

Facebook Groups can be secret (visible only to members), closed (anyone can see the group, but only members can post), or open (anyone can join instantly and post). Open groups tend to appeal mostly to spammers and marketers and in most cases are not a good investment of a nonprofit's time. Closed groups require that the admin approve all new members who request to join and are surprisingly powerful. All new group activity is featured under "Groups" on the news feed home page, and popular group posts are occasionally highlighted in the news feed. Since most Facebook users are very active, closed groups are a great way to organize small groups of people who have a common purpose and need to be in regular communication with one another. Unlike open and closed groups, secret groups do not show up in Graph Search results, but they have the same functionality as open and closed groups. If your nonprofit wants to organize staff, board members, volunteers, or activists beyond using email, Facebook Groups are an excellent alternative. It's also worth noting that for colleges and universities, Facebook also offers an advanced group tool set called "Groups for Schools."

FACEBOOK EVENTS

Facebook Events have fallen off the radar screen of most nonprofits primarily because event invitations do not automatically get news feed exposure and because admins can't invite fans directly to the event—only friends can invite friends to an event. However, once the event is created, you can then post the link to the event in a status update and ask your fans to RSVP and invite their friends to the event. Facebook Events also appear in searches that are locally based. Again, considering the power of friend-to-friend activity inside the Facebook community, nonprofits would be wise to take a second look at Facebook Events.

When creating an event, be sure to upload an event photo and tag the place where the event will be held. If the event is not free, you can include a link to your website where people can purchase tickets. It's also worth noting that events posted as a status update can be highlighted for increased exposure. Once an event page is created, attendees can post comments on it, and you can message, or chat, on a one-to-one basis with those who have RSVP'd. Nonprofits often post links to their website on Facebook to promote their events, but this doesn't allow for friends to invite friends or for Facebook search optimization. Thus, using Facebook Events in addition to regular promotion of your annual gala or other fundraising and community events can only help increase attendance rates. In fact, you may want to experiment with promoting your Facebook Event in email communications and on other social networks to increase your RSVP count and the possibility of friends inviting other friends.

FACEBOOK LOCATION

Originally launched as Facebook Places in 2010, Facebook renamed its geolocation and mapping service Facebook Location in 2011. Facebook Places was problematic in that when Facebook users checked in to a location, such as a museum, hospital, or library for the first time on their mobile device, a Facebook Places Page was created for that location separate from the official page of the museum, hospital, or library.

This resulted in a confusing and often frustrating conundrum in which nonprofits had multiple pages for their organization. Today, though unknown to many nonprofits since they rarely search for their own nonprofit on Facebook, many of those pages still exist and continue to be liked and checked into regularly. Thus, nonprofits need to do multiple searches on both facebook.com and inside of Facebook's mobile apps to discover if they have one or more Facebook Places Pages in existence and then request to merge them with your official page. You can request the merge directly on the Facebook Places Page itself. If your official page and the Places Page are *identical in name, or very similar*, the two will be merged, and your official page will then gain as fans those who had liked your Facebook Place Page. If the names are not identical or very similar, your request to merge will most likely be ignored.

Once your nonprofit merges your pages, your official page will then have the Facebook Location functionality added to the page. If you could not find duplicate Places Pages, you can add the location functionality to your page by simply entering a physical address in your admin panel. Your page will then be enabled with check-in and review functionality, a map will be added, and your page will begin to show up in local searches in Facebook mobile apps. For location-based nonprofits, such as performing arts venues, animal shelters, zoos, aquariums, universities, and churches, Facebook Location is a must-add functionality.

NONPROFITS TO STUDY AND LEARN FROM

❏ The Trevor Project: facebook.com/thetrevorproject

❏ People for the Ethical Treatment of Animals (PETA): facebook.com/officialpeta

❏ Doctors Without Borders: facebook.com/msf.english

❏ Amnesty International: facebook.com/amnestyglobal

❏ American Civil Liberties Union (ACLU): facebook.com/aclu.nationwide

10

Twitter

While Twitter has only one-third the number of active users that Facebook has, Twitter is one of the fastest-growing social networks in the world. As it continues to become more integrated into television entertainment and news, this trend will likely continue. Heavily used by the media, bloggers, and brands to distribute information and breaking news, Twitter prides itself on being an information network. Yes, there are individuals who tweet and socialize with one another, but for nonprofits the power of Twitter is primarily in using it as a distribution channel to build brand recognition and reputation. One of the greatest misperceptions about Twitter is that its effectiveness for nonprofits rests in chatting and having informal, personal conversations with followers. For customer service, this is relevant, but for building a brand and increasing the number of your followers, the data just don't back the assertion that "being human" on Twitter is the ultimate best practice.

Rather, nonprofits should make it a top priority to become an expert Twitter resource for information relevant to their mission and cause(s). People primarily follow your nonprofit on Twitter because they care about your cause and they want information, success stories, and thought-provoking content that they can retweet to their followers as an expression of support and activism. Twitter best practices for individuals need to be separated from those for nonprofit brands. An individual who wants to build a powerful personal brand on Twitter needs to chat and engage in discussions frequently, but a nonprofit brand does not. Blasphemous to many Twitter experts, there is nothing wrong with making distributing information on Twitter a higher priority than having conversations with your followers if you are a nonprofit brand. In fact, you may discover that focusing on content distribution is exactly the strategy that your nonprofit needs.

TWITTER FOR FUNDRAISING AND CAUSE AWARENESS

Fundraising tweets are generally the least retweeted tweets posted by nonprofits on Twitter. Creating a compelling fundraising ask in 140 characters is extremely challenging. Unless you have influential Twitterers (or you are an influential Twitterer) who will retweet your fundraising tweets or advocate that Twitterers donate to your nonprofit, it's better to rank fundraising asks low in your Twitter strategy. However, there are exceptions and times when Twitter can increase your online fundraising results tenfold.[1] This is during times of crisis and on cause awareness days (discussed in Chapter 15). Fundraising asks that foster a sense of urgency perform very well on Twitter—even text-to-give pitches—and are highly retweeted. On most days, however, your Twitter fundraising strategy needs to be more subtle. Like storytelling through status updates on Facebook, storytelling through tweets eventually converts some followers into donors.

TOP FIVE TWITTER BEST PRACTICES FOR NONPROFITS

It's impossible to apply Twitter best practices across all segments of the nonprofit sector because of the wide variety of causes and follower counts, but trends in scientific analysis of Twitter clearly indicate that there is a right way and a wrong way to use Twitter. The challenge is for nonprofits to learn from the data, adopt the data, and then adapt them to their Twitter strategy. It takes time to realize that Twitter is much more complicated and nuanced than it appears. However, if you study it, learn it well, and grow to enjoy it, then your time invested will eventually pay off through increased brand recognition, referral traffic, new donors, volunteers, event attendees, and possibly even media coverage.

1. Think of Your Followers First

Again, people follow nonprofits on Twitter primarily because they are interested in the causes that each nonprofit advocates. This fact should always be first and foremost in your mind when developing your Twitter strategy. If the majority of your tweets are focused on fundraising (Donate to us!) and marketing (Follow us on Facebook!), then you will struggle to gain followers and build momentum on Twitter because most of those tweets are ignored.

It is crucial that the person tweeting on behalf of your nonprofit gains a sense of who your followers are and what kind of content inspires them to promote and interact with your nonprofit on Twitter through retweets, mentions, favorites, and click-throughs. Silence speaks volumes on Twitter and if your "@Connect" tab is devoid of activity, then it's time to change the type of content your nonprofit has been tweeting. As a general rule, especially in the first few months of using Twitter, ask yourself, "Would my followers find this interesting?" If your first instinct is no, then don't tweet it. Over time as you get a better understanding of the kind of content that your Twitter community expects from you, your ability to cut through the noise, stand out from the clutter, and gain influence on Twitter will expand.

2. Make Getting Retweeted a Priority

Evan Williams, one of the cofounders of Twitter, believes that influence on Twitter is best measured by how often a brand or individual gets retweeted.[2] Unfortunately, many nonprofits have yet to master or even consider how to make their tweets retweetable. It's a remarkable experience, however, once a nonprofit tweaks its Twitter strategy to focus on getting retweeted. First, by default, it just makes nonprofits better at Twitter. Poorly formatted, boring tweets do not get retweeted. Intelligent, inspirational, and well-formatted tweets do. Second, when retweeted, your @Connect tab will come alive with notifications of retweets, new followers, favorites, mentions, and being listed. And third, since retweets inspire activity, they also increase your nonprofit's exposure to potential new followers which consequently results in increased followers, brand recognition, and click-throughs to your website or blog.

The number of retweets your tweet will receive is highest within the first 10 minutes of posting, and this is true whether you have 1,000 or 100,000 followers.[3] If no retweets occur within the first 10 minutes that a tweet goes live, then it's unlikely to be retweeted in large numbers, and you need to question what it is about the tweet that made it unretweetable so you don't make the same mistake again. There is a social science to using Twitter and studying what people react to—and what they don't—is an attribute found in only the best Twitterers. In terms of content, powerful stats, inspirational quotes, visually compelling images, and news-related tweets with links are the most retweeted. It's also worth noting that adding "Please Retweet" has proven to generate four times as many retweets than when this is not added.[4] To improve your retweet research and your retweet rates, RetweetLab (retweetlab.com) and RetweetRank (retweetrank.com) are free services that can provide your nonprofit with detailed information on how many times you have been retweeted and on what days and during which hours you are retweeted most often.

Finally, it's also important to understand the power of retweeting others. If your nonprofit does not create a large amount of quality content, then curating the content of others through retweets is a wise Twitter strategy. This is going to require that your nonprofit drop the antiquated idea that promoting others detracts your followers from your nonprofit because, in truth, those who post and curate the most interesting, compelling content on Twitter are the most successful.

3. Format Your Tweets for Easy Reading
and to Increase Retweets

Your followers are much more likely to read and retweet your tweets if they are formatted for easy reading. This means the use of proper grammar, correct punctuation, no misspellings, no abbreviations, and complete succinct sentences. It also helps to limit your tweets to 130 characters and to put a colon after the last word before a link. Doing so results in higher click-through rates and retweets.[5] Mentioning others within a tweet by using the "@" symbol in front of a Twitter username in a tweet can also positively affect your retweet and click-through rates as well as foster collaboration and partnership on Twitter.

4. Use Twitter Lists and Twitter Favorites
and Follow Them Wisely

Many nonprofits new to Twitter mass follow in the hopes of getting mass followed in return, but it never works. Instead it sends a message of desperation and possibly that your account is a spam bot. The vast majority will not follow you in return, and essentially your debut on Twitter was doomed from the start. As a general rule, nonprofits should never follow more than they are being followed. If your nonprofit has been mass followed, then mass unfollow and start over.

Conversely, if your nonprofit follows very few Twitterers (e.g., you follow only 30, but have 5,000 followers), then you need to consider following more accounts. The more you follow, the more often your account is listed in "Followers" tabs and under the @Connect tab of those you follow. Twitterers want to be followed and being overly selective about following is counterproductive and limits your reach inside of Twitter. Of those nonprofits that choose to follow few accounts, they usually do so because they do not want to clutter their "Home" feed, but creating lists to organize your followers eliminates the problem of being inundated with tweets. Listing in and of itself is valuable to your nonprofit in that those who are listed receive notification that they have been listed, and they appreciate it. Your support is duly noted. Following and listing are simple ways to make connections with others inside Twitter.

However, be sure to follow strategically. For example, if you have 500 followers, then follow 200 foundations, individual and corporate donors, partner organizations, and local media. Then when you achieve 1,000 followers, follow 200 more and organize those 400 Twitterers into lists. If they follow in return, you don't need to thank them for following. Instead tweet an intelligent, authentic reply or send a direct message to the most important of your new followers. Mass thanking is an antiquated best practice that has been done many times over and thus no longer makes an impact. Also, under no circumstances should you automate direct messages (DMs) to new followers. Automated DMs have evolved to become perceived as spam, and this makes a terrible first impression on your new followers.

Finally, favoriting tweets is one of the least used functions of Twitter, but an incredibly useful one. Quite often you'll find a tweet that you want to retweet later or that includes content that you want to research and possibly share on other social networks. Favoriting these tweets adds them to your "Favorites" tab, which then allows you to keep a working to-do list of the tweets that you want to retweet or research. Once a tweet is retweeted or researched, simply unfavorite the tweet, and it is removed from your Favorites tab. Additionally, when you favorite a tweet, the account that tweeted the tweet is notified in its @Connect tab. Don't underestimate the power of your account showing up in the @Connect tab of other accounts, whether that's through following, retweeting, mentioning, replying, favoriting, or listing. Little actions get noticed on Twitter and are often reciprocated.

5. Tweet or Retweet Every Two Hours, in the Evenings, and on the Weekends

More than any other best practice, it's difficult and often controversial to state how often a nonprofit should tweet. Facebook pulls your status updates out of the news feed if you post too often. On Twitter, every tweet goes to the home feed. Finding the balance between not annoying your followers with too many tweets and posting just the right amount to keep them interested and retained as followers is challenging. To illuminate this point, consider how you react to those nonprofits who tweet hourly or more. Most Twitterers begin to tune out or unfollow them. This is a Twitter reality that your nonprofit wants to avoid. Most often, a tweet has a 60- to 120-minute lifespan so by posting only every two hours, your nonprofit maximizes your follower growth and retention rates as well as your retweetability. Data on click-through rates validate that tweeting once every two hours is an optimal frequency for most nonprofit brands. When you tweet every two hours, your click-through rate increases by 300 percent while it drops to an average of only 70 percent when you tweet hourly. Thereafter, the click-through rates plummet to barely above zero.[6] Test tweeting every hour for a week and monitor your growth rate. If it stagnates or drops, you're losing followers from tweeting too often. If it grows, then your tweets are so excellent and thus your retweet rate so high that followers are gained by this level of activity. Odds are, however, that you'll find that posting every two hours (a tweet or a retweet) is the best frequency. If you can't be that active on Twitter, a minimum of two or three tweets or retweets a day is required for Twitter success.

Twitter is most active from 8 a.m. to 12 noon. Therefore, your nonprofit should focus on tweeting during the morning hours. However, it's difficult to stand out from the millions of other tweets being posted during that time. This is why some of the highest interaction rates occur in the afternoon and evenings, and on the weekends. Retweets and click-throughs are often higher in the afternoon and evening and exceptionally high on Saturday and Sunday mornings. Data have pinpointed that 2:30 p.m. and 8 p.m. are the optimal times for retweets during the work week and that tweets posted at noon and 6 p.m. produce the highest click-through rates.[7] While these data are useful and meant to inspire you to experiment with tweeting at various times throughout the day, it's important to know that these data fluctuate wildly. If suddenly a large number of Twitterers begin posting at 2:30 p.m., then that time loses its power because a sudden increase in the volume of tweets makes it more challenging for your tweets to get noticed. If your nonprofit does not want to be active during evening hours or on the weekends, social media dashboards such as HootSuite (hootsuite.com) and TweetDeck (tweetdeck .com) allow you to schedule tweets and retweets in advance, and Twitter is likely to add a native scheduling function in the future as well.

10 TWITTER HASHTAGS FOR NONPROFITS

Hashtags can be a powerful way to gain exposure for your nonprofit on Twitter, but only if they are used wisely and with authenticity. The overuse of hashtags is a rampant problem and is counterproductive to getting retweeted. In fact, using more than one or two hashtags per tweet has been proven to drop interactions by 17 percent.[8] Thus, to avoid becoming labeled a hashtag spammer and to ensure that your nonprofit's tweets consistently get retweeted, it's crucial that you limit yourself to using only one or two hashtags per tweet—and not in every tweet.

1. Create Your Own Hashtags for Campaigns and Events

The best use of hashtags on Twitter is when they are created for awareness and fundraising campaigns and events. For example, if your nonprofit works on women's issues or international development, many nonprofits use the hashtag #IWD to tap into the flurry of activity that occurs on Twitter in the weeks leading up to International Women's Day on March 8 of every year. Or if your nonprofit is launching its own awareness campaign, such as the World Wildlife Fund's #StopWildlifeCrime campaign, then create a unique hashtag and promote the hashtag on your website, in your blog, in your e-newsletter, and on social networks. Then have a page on your website that explains what the hashtag represents and how supporters should use it. If your campaign is to be an annual event, then use the same hashtag year after year. As the hashtag becomes more well-known and widely used, your nonprofit benefits from being the originator.

For conferences and other events, creating a unique hashtag is ideal so that those in attendance can tweet live during the event and so those who cannot attend can follow the event through the tweets using the hashtag. For example, the Nonprofit Technology Enterprise Network (NTEN) uses the hashtag #NTC for its annual conference, but with the year attached for each conference; thus #14NTC is for the 2014 conference. The hashtag is promoted in all conference materials, both print and online, and becomes more popular with each passing year, which consequently increases referral traffic, Twitter followers, and brand recognition for NTEN.

2. Use Hashtags That Are Related to Your Mission and Programs

The more general your hashtags, the more likely your tweets will be retweeted. Keep it simple and focus on the big picture. For example, if you are a nonprofit that advocates for college access, use the hashtag #Education. An organization that advocates marriage equality? Use #LGBT. Don't fracture the power of hashtags or decrease your retweetability by using overly specific hashtags. When in doubt, search the hashtag before using it. If there is little to no activity, then use a different hashtag or none at all.

3. Use Hashtags That Are Related to Breaking News and Current Events

Every day there are breaking news and current events stories that are being widely discussed and debated by the media and bloggers on Twitter. If your nonprofit's mission or programs are related to any of the stories, then tap into the power of the hashtags being most widely used in association with the breaking news and current events stories. For example, poverty organizations should monitor and use when appropriate the hashtags #MinimumWage or #Hunger. If you are an environmental organization, then monitor and use the hashtags #Green and #ClimateChange. As a best practice, research and monitor the 10 keyword hashtags most relevant to your mission and programs and use them on the days when they are being widely used. If you format your tweets for retweeting and have a bit of luck and good timing, your tweet may trend to become a "Top" tweet in hashtag search results.

4. Use the Hashtag of Your City and State

For location-based events or current affairs relevant to your local or state community, using the hashtag of your city or state can help your nonprofit get noticed by Twitterers in your area, thus increasing the likelihood of your gaining new event attendees, volunteers, and donors.

5. #Nonprofit, #Charity, and #NGO

In North America, "nonprofit" is the term most used to define the philanthropic sector. In Europe and Australia, it's "charity," and in most developing nations, it's "non-governmental organization," or "NGO." All three hashtags—#Nonprofit, #Charity, and #NGO—are widely monitored and used on Twitter. When discussing your mission and programs, occasionally hashtag your tweets with one of these three hashtags depending on your location. Also if you are a global organization, use all three relevant to the time zones during which you are tweeting.

6. #NPTech

Short for "nonprofit technology," #NPTech is a hashtag that is used to tag advice and best practices in nonprofit technology. Rarely tweeted by nonprofits, #NPTech is a useful hashtag for following the most current information on topics ranging from CRMs to smartphone apps.

7. #Fundraising and #Philanthropy

The #Fundraising and #Philanthropy hashtags provide access to information about current trends in fundraising and philanthropy. The #Fundraising hashtag is most often used to tag case studies or discuss new fundraising tools, while #Philanthropy tends to showcase tweets related to donor behavior and grantmaking.

8. #Mobile

Nonprofits have been slow to adopt the #Mobile hashtag. For all things related to mobile websites, mobile fundraising, and mobile marketing trends, regularly monitoring the #Mobile hashtag is a wise and useful investment of your time.

9. #Volunteer

If your nonprofit has volunteer positions open, using the #Volunteer hashtag can help you gain access to both virtual and in-person volunteers. The hashtag is also useful for thanking volunteers and monitoring trends in volunteerism.

10. #CharityTuesday and #FundraisingFriday

Nonprofits should get in the habit of using the #CharityTuesday and #FundraisingFriday hashtag on a regular basis. On #CharityTuesdays Twitterers promote their favorite nonprofits (charities and NGOs), and on #FundraisingFriday Twitterers are asked to donate to one of their favorite nonprofits. To maximize your success, create a page on your website or blog that explains how the hashtags are meant to be used, and list specific actions that Twitterers can take on behalf of your nonprofit on #CharityTuesday(s) and #FundraisingFriday(s). Then, early in the morning on each Tuesday and Friday, post a tweet using the hashtag and a link to your #CharityTuesday and #FundraisingFriday pages.

HOW TO HOST A TWEET CHAT FOR YOUR NONPROFIT

The rise of Twitter has resulted in a new campaign awareness strategy and online event known as a tweet chat. Organized around the use of a hashtag, such as #HealthTalk or #PovertyChat, nonprofits worldwide are adding tweet chats to their editorial calendars. Scheduled to occur at a specific time for usually an hour or less, nonprofits use Twitter to have live conversations on topics relevant to their mission and programs. When done well, nonprofits can gain exposure on Twitter, solidify their brand as an expert resource, and increase awareness about the issues they advocate.

Some large nonprofits host tweet chats monthly, while others do so only during the launch of specific campaigns or case studies. Unlike normal tweeting when tweeting or retweeting every two hours is optimal, during tweet chats nonprofits can tweet and retweet as often as they wish—provided that the tweets and retweets are well-formatted, useful, and, of course, relevant to the tweet chat. To ensure a successful tweet chat, nonprofits should:

- Create a hashtag specifically themed to the topic of the tweet chat.

- Schedule the tweet chat at least one month in advance and create a page on their website or blog that details the date, time, and topic and highlights their nonprofit's Twitter username, the tweet chat hashtag, and special guests that will participate in the tweet chat (include their Twitter usernames and avatars).

- Use a tweet chat tool such as Twubs (twubs.com) to create branded tweet chat rooms or Storify (storify.com) to chronicle the tweet chat after it's over.

- In the weeks leading up to the tweet chat, promote the tweet chat on all communication channels.

- On the days leading up to the tweet chat, promote the event at least once daily on Twitter. In the hours immediately before the start of your tweet chat, post hourly reminders. This will help increase your attendance rate and warn those who do not want to attend that their home feed will likely be inundated with tweets from your nonprofit during the tweet chat thus lessoning the likelihood that they will unfollow you for tweeting too often.

- Prewrite at least 10 tweets that you can post during lulls in order to increase engagement, such as powerful stats, inspirational quotes, and thought-provoking questions.

- Encourage attendees to share resources relevant to the tweet chat and to upload photos and infographics during the tweet chat for a more visual experience.

- Poll your attendees during tweet chats using TwtPoll (twtpoll .com).

- Write a follow-up article or blog post that highlights the 10 most popular tweets from the tweet chat, and list at least three actions that attendees of the tweet chat can take, such as signing up for an e-newsletter, signing an online petition, or making a donation. If you have another tweet chat scheduled, list the details and then promote the follow-up article across all your social networks.

NONPROFITS TO STUDY AND LEARN FROM

❑ Oxfam International: twitter.com/oxfam

❑ Natural Resources Defense Council (NRDC): twitter.com/nrdc

❑ Idealist: twitter.com/idealist

❑ Gates Foundation: twitter.com/gatesfoundation

❑ Acumen Fund: twitter.com/acumen

11

Google+

L aunched in June 2011, Google+ had high hopes of wooing away Facebook users and becoming the predominant online social network. The problem with the Google+ launch, however, was that it launched without having brand pages in place, and thus the early adopter nonprofits (and businesses) had very little interest in using or promoting Google+ until they could create their own page. Trying to launch solely as social network for individuals rather than as a social network for individuals and brands was a mistake that cost Google+ much of the excitement and buzz that was generated in the months leading up to and the weeks after the launch.

By the time Google+ released brand pages five months after launch, many nonprofits had already converted individual profiles into brand profiles and did not want to start over with creating a brand page, some were just downright confused by the process of signing up and becoming active on Google+ as a nonprofit, and others simply lost interest. Nonetheless, the early adopter nonprofits that rode out the rough launch of Google+ and who have been consistently active on the site since are starting to experience payoff. The National Wildlife Federation, for example, now has more followers on Google+ than on Facebook and Twitter combined despite their using Facebook and Twitter twice as long as they've used Google+.

Today, Google+ is a growing social network with an extensive tool set for brand pages that at the very least rivals Facebook, and many Google+ users would say surpasses it. In fact, many nonprofits that know how to use Google+ effectively are reporting engagement rates equal to, and sometimes surpassing, their Facebook and Twitter engagement rates. As Google continues to weave Google+ into its entire suite of products ranging from Gmail to Google Search to YouTube, not using Google+ could become problematic for your nonprofit in the years to come.

GOOGLE+ FOR FUNDRAISING AND CAUSE AWARENESS

Like any other social network, fundraising is a challenge because you cannot easily track your donor activity. Google Wallet and Google's One Today mobile fundraising app could prove to be very powerful for those nonprofits pioneering Google+. As discussed in Chapter 6, mobile wallets that also enable online donations are going to transform online giving as we know it. Of all the mobile wallet services, Google Wallet has placed more emphasis on helping nonprofits fundraise than any other wallet service. Integration of Google Wallet and Google's One Today app into Google+ Pages will heavily benefit those nonprofits that have invested time in building their Google+ Communities, and that donor activity will be trackable. In terms of cause awareness, the content your nonprofit posts that receives the most +1s receives increased exposure inside both Google+ and Google Search which then ultimately results in higher awareness for the cause(s) your nonprofit advocates for and increased exposure of your Google+ Page.

TOP FIVE GOOGLE+ BEST PRACTICES FOR NONPROFITS

Google+ has many hidden features and unique functionalities that require hours of exploring and experimenting with to fully comprehend them. Thus far, most nonprofits have taken a rather haphazard approach to Google+. They post their obligatory link for the day or week, and that's it. No monitoring, no engagement, and no exploring of the tool set. Google has every intention of making its social network popular worldwide, and for that fact alone nonprofits would be wise to take Google+ seriously. From being able to edit an update after it's posted to recording video updates directly from Google+ to viewing "Ripples" of how content spreads throughout Google+, nonprofits should allot at least an hour or two weekly to becoming more familiar with its tool set, understanding how the Google+ Community is unique, and then implementing a Google+ strategy that ensures success.

1. Make Visuals a Priority

The Google+ interface is more visual than Facebook or Twitter. When posted, photos and videos are much larger and thus more eye-catching. The pages themselves display content in a Pinterest-like format. For your nonprofit to be successful on Google+, you need visual content. Most nonprofits simply share links as updates to Google+, and the vast majority of those updates are ignored as indicated by their low +1 rates. Thus, similar to Facebook, the best update strategy on Google+ is to include a brief message and link inside the body of the update, remove the automated link and image, and then directly upload and share the photo associated with the message and link. This method of sharing ensures that your updates are more visible in the Google+ Stream and thus more likely to receive interaction and engagement.

When sharing, also be sure to include a hashtag. Similar to your Twitter hashtag strategy, your hashtags should be general and not too obscure. You should also regularly monitor the hashtag pages for #nonprofit, #nptech, #mobile, and so on. Quite often you'll discover some of the best nonprofit technology content on Google+ since many early adopter mobile and social media experts tend to be very active on Google+ because they relish pioneering a new community.

Finally, in terms of content, an effective Google+ strategy is similar to that on other social networks. Focus on storytelling, know your tone of voice, resist the urge to use Google+ primarily as a marketing tool, share powerful stats and inspirational quotes in a visual format, monitor discussion, engage authentically, and always have it in the back of your mind that behind every Google+ avatar is a human being who wants to be inspired. Provided that you always put the interests of your community first, referral traffic, increased brand recognition, and donor and supporter conversions will follow.

2. Regularly +1 the Content of Others

Your nonprofit benefits from receiving +1s on Google+, but giving +1s is also an easy way to gain exposure. With every +1 given, your page's avatar is attached to the update you +1ed, and with more than any other social network, that simple act leads to more followers and reciprocated +1s. Google+ users pay attention to who is +1ing and the page upon which you +1 an update receives a notification that your nonprofit has +1ed their update. Thus, taking a couple of minutes a day to +1 five or six updates posted by partner nonprofits, funders, or news sources is a minimal time investment that when consistently done over time ensures steady growth of your Google+ Community. Also, when followers post a comment on your page, that comment can be +1ed, and +1ing comments posted by your followers is a simple way to say, "Thanks for the comment!" (the commenter is notified of your +1) without actually having to say the now-too-often-said, "Thanks for the comment!" As a general rule on social networks, once a best practice reaches critical mass, it begins to become monotonous, and at that point it's time to start thinking outside the box and try something different.

3. Merge Your YouTube Channel with Your Google+ Page

Google owns YouTube. When you sign up for a new YouTube channel, you are now prompted to sign up for a Google account. Your new Google account also contains a new Google+ personal profile (from which you create your nonprofit's Google+ Page) and Gmail account as well as a new YouTube channel. Nonprofits that created YouTube channels before this change in 2012 can request to merge their YouTube channel with their Google+ Page. To do so, go to your YouTube settings and follow the instructions to connect your Google+ Page with your YouTube channel. Once completed, your Google+ Page will have a new tab called "YouTube" that includes all the videos you have uploaded to YouTube.

For those nonprofits that have long-standing Google accounts, the process of merging is more complicated because two Google accounts cannot currently be merged. This fact compounded the frustration and confusion many had during the launch of Google+. At some point, you'll be able to have all your Google products under one account. In the meantime you'll have to have two accounts. Google+ Help provides excellent up-to-date how-tos on recent upgrades to both Google accounts and Google+.

4. Optimize Your Page for Google Search

In April 2013 Google changed its search results so that nonprofit Google+ Pages are featured prominently in Google Search results. To ensure that your nonprofit's page is optimized for Google Search, you must request to link your Google+ Page to your website and enter a tagline and introduction. All three can be done in the "About" section of your Google+ Page. Additionally, Google Search pulls information about your nonprofit from Wikipedia and GuideStar (guidestar.org), so make certain that your Wikipedia entry is up to date and that your GuideStar nonprofit report is updated annually. Finally, by sharing content regularly on your Google+ Page, your most recent update will be featured in Google Search results along with the avatar of your nonprofit and your follower count.

5. Share Three to Four Times Weekly

Unlike Facebook, all the content your nonprofit shares on Google+ is published to the stream. Google+ does not have an algorithm that determines what content is worthy of publication. The guarantee of exposure is clearly positive and frees you from endless hours of trying to game an algorithm. At the same time this means that your nonprofit's updates could be easily missed on Google+, especially if your followers follow many individuals and pages. To maximize Google+, you can post up to twice daily—once in the morning and once in the afternoon, or even a third time in the evening. Your minimal requirement, however, is to share content three to four times weekly. Experiment with different days and times and monitor your interaction and engagement rates. Weekends tend to be very quiet on Google+, but as the site continues to gain more users, this could change. As Google+ continues to grow, an algorithm may be in its future. Nothing kills a social network faster than spam and clutter, so at the point where the stream becomes overly inundated with content, Google+ may have to implement an algorithm to ensure that only the most interesting content is published to the stream.

GOOGLE+ COMMUNITIES

Like Facebook and LinkedIn Groups, Google+ Communities are meant to organize groups of people who share common interests. Launched in December 2012, communities can be private or open. For nonprofits, the power is currently in creating or participating in open groups. Until large numbers of people are regularly active on Google+, your nonprofit will likely struggle with using communities to organize volunteers, board members, and staff, but if you are eager and willing to invest more time in Google+, communities are worth experimenting with.

A good first step to acquaint your nonprofit with Google+ Communities is to browse and join a couple of large groups relevant to your mission and programs. For example, nonprofits that advocate for animal welfare or wildlife conservation should join "Animals" or "Wildlife" communities and share updates and branded photos. They can then monitor their updates for interaction and engagement. You may be very surprised to discover that the updates you share in communities receive more +1s and comments than those you post on your own page. Unless a Google+ user specifically requests in their personal settings that community updates not be shared in their stream, your community updates will be seen by hundreds, and possibly thousands, of Google+ users who are not currently following your page. By becoming active in a select number of communities on a regular basis, your page will gain new followers, and the content you share will move up in the ranks of Google Search.

As far as creating a Google+ Community is concerned, only large nonprofits with national or international brand recognition have been successful at building communities that are titled with the name of their nonprofit. A better strategy for those nonprofits that want to experiment with Google+ Communities would be to create a community that is more generally titled. For example, if your nonprofit works in international development, create a community called "International Development" or "Global Health" and then invite the followers of your nonprofit's page to join your community. For regional nonprofits, consider creating a group such as "Nonprofits in San Francisco" or "Philanthropy in Denver." If you get lucky and create a group that has mass appeal by showing up often in communities search results, being the admin of a Google+ Community comes with many perks. Your nonprofit's page is featured as the creator, you can list your nonprofit's website and social networks on the Community home page, you can use a photo to represent your community that's branded with your nonprofit's avatar, and not to be underestimated, your nonprofit becomes perceived as a leader—whether that's in "International Development" or in "Philanthropy in Denver."

GOOGLE+ EVENTS

Google+ Events are gaining momentum. Although they are mostly used by nonprofits to promote Google+ Hangouts, now is a good time to start adding Google+ Events to your event promotion strategy. Whether it's a gala, a tweet chat, or an open house, Google+ Events can be created in less than 10 minutes and can be shared with followers, circles, and communities that can then also share the event with their followers and communities. Even if Google+ never goes mainstream, there are currently enough active users on the site to make Google Events worth the time investment.

When creating an event, be sure to upload a custom banner, list all the details of your event, and add a map. If your nonprofit has a

Google+ Local Page, you can tag it directly when creating your event. You can also add a link to your website where tickets can be purchased and a YouTube video. Be sure to regularly monitor your event because attendees and prospective attendees often post questions and comments, and one of the most unique features of Google+ Events is that attendees can also add photos taken at the event in real-time using a Google+ mobile app or after the event using their PCs. It's also worth noting that when a Google+ user RSVPs to an event, the event is then added to the user's Google Calendar.

GOOGLE+ PLACES

For many years a Google search of a nonprofit that was locally based resulted in a Google map that linked to the nonprofit's Google Places Page. A nonprofit could claim its places page, update contact and location information, monitor reviews, upload photos, and view analytics for their Google Places Page. However, indicative of Google's long-term commitment to Google+, in May 2012 all Places Pages were converted into Google+ Local Pages. If you have not recently searched for your nonprofit on Google, you may be surprised to discover that your nonprofit now has a Google+ Local Page. The easiest way to find your local page is to visit plus.google.com/local and search for your nonprofit. If your nonprofit does not already have a Google+ Local account, then request to verify your Google+ Local Page and complete the sign-up process for Google+ Local.

Location-based nonprofits cannot ignore Google+ Local Pages (or Facebook Location) because Google+ users can write reviews, upload photos, +1 your local page, and check in to your local page using Google+ mobile apps. While the +1 activity and check-in activity are low compared to Facebook Location check-ins and likes, Google now accounts for 25 percent of all Internet usage in North America—more than Facebook, Netflix, and Instagram combined.[1] At some point Google+ will enable the functionality to merge your Google+ Local Page with your official page, and as always, the early adopters will benefit the most.

GOOGLE+ HANGOUTS

The ability to host live video conferences for thousands of donors and supporters at no cost has lured many nonprofits to Google+. Known as Google+ Hangouts On Air, nonprofits can broadcast a live video conference directly from their Google+ Page. After the conference is over, a recording of the event is then uploaded to the nonprofits' YouTube channel. By creating a Google+ "Circle" of speakers, only those added to the speakers circle will be visible and audible during the hangout, while all other followers simply watch and listen to the conference and submit questions and comments during the hangout through the Google+ Hangout On Air event invitation and chat module. To ensure a successful hangout on air, nonprofits should:

- Do a test Google+ Hangout On Air with staff to familiarize yourself with the hangout tool set.

- Create a Google+ Event and invite all your followers to RSVP.

- Create a website article that links to the invitation and your Google+ Page and informs people that they must be a Google+ user to view the Hangout On Air and then promote the article across all online communication channels at least one month before the hangout is to occur.

- Repost the event invitation on your Google+ Page at least once a week during the month leading up to the hangout as well as the day before and the day of the hangout.

- Create a hashtag specifically themed on the topic of the hangout for increased exposure both before and during the hangout.

- Select a moderator for the hangout who is comfortable with public speaking. Be sure to have questions and topics for discussion written in advance to ensure an interesting and engaging hangout. Panelists should also be comfortable with public speaking and be encouraged to participate in the hangout while on location using a Google+ mobile app.

- Share your desktop during the hangout and feature PowerPoint slides that showcase powerful stats and images relevant to the topic of your hangout.

- Ensure that a staff person is available to moderate and answer questions posted on your event invitation and in the chat room during the hangout. You can also post comments and questions and share resources to encourage attendee participation.

- Follow up your hangout with a website article or blog post that includes the recording of your hangout, the top five takeaways from it, and a call to action. Then promote the article or blog post on all online communication channels. If you have another Google+ Hangout On Air already scheduled, then link it to the invitation so readers can RSVP.

A successful Google+ Hangout On Air can lead to hundreds or possibly thousands of new Google+ followers and position your nonprofit to be on the cutting edge of nonprofit technology. In addition to Google+ Hangouts On Air, your nonprofit can also host Google+ Hangouts for up to 10 people. Primarily used to hold virtual staff meetings or to organize volunteers, Google+ Hangouts differ from Google+ Hangouts On Air in that they are not broadcast live on your Google+ Page, and they are not recorded on YouTube.

NONPROFITS TO STUDY AND LEARN FROM

- ❑ Zoo Atlanta: plus.google.com/+zooatlanta

- ❑ New York Public Library: plus.google.com/+newyorkpubliclibrary

- ❑ KQED Science: plus.google.com/+kqedscience

- ❑ American Heart Association: plus.google.com/+americanheart

- ❑ American Association of Retired Persons (AARP): plus.google .com/+aarp

12

LinkedIn

E very second two new members sign up for LinkedIn. With more than 250 million members in over 200 countries and territories, LinkedIn has positioned itself as *the* social network for professionals. Unlike other social networks that focus on an individual's personal life, LinkedIn focuses on its users' work experience, accolades, awards, and one-to-one online networking skills. Used by most nonprofit professionals, LinkedIn is a social network utilized primarily for work, not for socializing with friends and family.

Savvy nonprofit professionals who excel in online professional networking can use LinkedIn to build their personal brands, engage with board members and major donors, and secure new partnerships with other nonprofits and businesses. LinkedIn's unique membership and tool set make it an ideal social network where entrepreneurial individuals can thrive and in the process make some very important connections on behalf of their nonprofits. Using LinkedIn as a communication channel for your nonprofit is challenging. LinkedIn itself understands the value of content distribution, and the company is moving in that direction through the continued improvement of LinkedIn Pages. However, compared to Facebook, Twitter, and Google+, the rewards of using LinkedIn to distribute your nonprofit's content are not as immediate.

LINKEDIN FOR FUNDRAISING AND
CAUSE AWARENESS

If LinkedIn members become as active as they are on other social networks, then LinkedIn will be transformed into a more powerful tool for increasing awareness about the cause(s) your nonprofit advocates. College students and recent college graduates are the fastest-growing demographic on LinkedIn and since they often seek internships as a means of securing full-time employment, LinkedIn is also an obvious fit for recruiting qualified interns and volunteers. As far as fundraising is concerned, there are few data concerning Linked Groups or LinkedIn Pages resulting in significant dollars raised. But as the company continues to evolve and place more emphasis on content distribution and with more than 1.6 million nonprofits in the United States alone, any social networking company would be wise to offer tailored services for the nonprofit sector. It wouldn't be surprising if at some point in the future nonprofits will be able to add donate buttons and crowdfunding options to their LinkedIn Pages. In terms of corporate social responsibility, offering nonprofits a more customized tool set is a wise a strategy and in an Internet age where social good is highly valued across all sectors, LinkedIn has great potential for connecting nonprofits with corporate and small business funders.

TOP FIVE LINKEDIN
BEST PRACTICES FOR NONPROFITS

For nonprofits that want to expand their LinkedIn strategy beyond personal professional networking, LinkedIn Company Pages should be your top priority. Launched in 2010, the LinkedIn Page tool set has expanded slowly. It wasn't until 2013 that nonprofits started to pay serious attention to LinkedIn Pages and sharing updates on a regular basis. The results thus far have been mixed. Unless your nonprofit makes a concerted effort to promote your LinkedIn Page both inside LinkedIn and on other communication channels, it's a challenge to grow a community large enough to gain significant referral traffic and interaction and engagement rates equal to those of other social networks. However, LinkedIn's advertising model is built upon making LinkedIn Pages a success, and without a doubt the tool set will continue to expand in the hope of incentivizing both nonprofits and businesses to use LinkedIn Pages more consistently in their content strategies. Provided you don't expect instantaneous results, investing the time to brand and set up your page and build your following could prove to be very beneficial in the future. LinkedIn has an excellent reputation and the best customer service of any of the most well-known social networks. When you combine these with the company's new focus on becoming a content distribution site, LinkedIn Pages have all the makings of a success story for nonprofits.

1. Add Products and Services and Request Recommendations

As the predominate social network for professionals, it's imperative that your nonprofit's LinkedIn Page make a strong first impression. In addition to a custom-designed banner, you should also have custom-designed graphics for the products and services that you add to your page. When setting up your page, fill out every field applicable, and if you have a well-produced video that summarizes your nonprofit's mission and programs, add it to your page. Before launching your page to the public, you should ensure that each of your products and services has at least one recommendation. You can send recommendation requests to your personal connections directly inside LinkedIn, or send an email to key supporters and donors asking them to provide recommendations. LinkedIn notifies you how often your products and services are viewed, and it's often enough to require a concerted effort to get recommendations.

2. Encourage Staff to Promote Your LinkedIn Page to Their Connections

All staff should be encouraged to add their current work experience to their personal profiles. Doing so will feature your nonprofit's LinkedIn Page on their profiles and results in an announcement being sent to the news feed that links to your nonprofit's page. In addition, to help grow your page's following, ask staff to periodically share your page with their connections. Volunteers and board members should also be encouraged to add their "Volunteer Experience & Causes" to their profiles to increase exposure of your nonprofit on LinkedIn. It's important to understand that all staff, volunteer, and board activity on LinkedIn is attached to your nonprofit's page, so the more active they are inside LinkedIn, the more exposure your nonprofit receives.

3. Experiment with LinkedIn Jobs

Idealist (idealist.org) is the best known job posting service for the nonprofit sector and is highly recommended. But investing in LinkedIn job postings could expose your nonprofit to a new pool of highly qualified candidates. The postings are featured on your LinkedIn Page and promoted in job search results and email notifications. Discounts can be applied for, and for those nonprofits that want to use LinkedIn for recruiting board members and volunteers, LinkedIn offers free and discounted services through their LinkedIn for Good program (nonprofit .linkedin.com).

4. Regularly Monitor Your LinkedIn Analytics

Linked pages offer extensive page analytics. You can compare the engagement and click-through rates of your updates and thus gain a better understanding of what kind of content your followers respond to. You can also track your growth rate over time, your reach, and the total number of page views. LinkedIn is very generous with the data it provides, and if you regularly monitor your analytics, a successful LinkedIn content strategy can be achieved in a relatively short time.

5. Share Two to Three Times Weekly

At a minimum your nonprofit should share updates two to three times weekly. That's an optimal number to be consistently active without oversharing. As your community grows and thus your interaction and engagement rates rise, you may discover that posting more often is a good frequency for your nonprofit. LinkedIn Pages have not yet been scientifically studied in the way that those of Facebook and Twitter have been, so you'll have to let your community guide you on how often you should share. If you get little to no interaction and engagement on your updates, then posting twice weekly is enough. You may not yet have the volume of followers necessary to require sharing more often, or you haven't yet discovered the type of content your LinkedIn followers respond to. Many nonprofits don't realize that they can attach photos to updates by selecting "Attach a File" and, like all other social networks, photos published in the news feed get higher interaction and engagement rates. Finally, all updates should include a well-formatted and smartly written message with a link.

LINKEDIN GROUPS

For many years nonprofits used LinkedIn Groups to build a brand and community inside of LinkedIn. With the rise of LinkedIn Pages, groups are experiencing slower growth rates. There's also a growing frustration on the part of LinkedIn Group members with the often overwhelming amount of marketing spam being posted in groups by fake accounts and overzealous marketers. Unless you diligently block and remove spammers, your members will begin to ignore or leave your group. It's possible that LinkedIn could launch new group functionalities in the future that reenergize members to join and participate more often in groups, but the company itself is heavily emphasizing pages over groups. On the social web, some tools become obsolete over time as new trends emerge as was the case with Facebook Pages surpassing Facebook Groups in popularity.

That's not to say that LinkedIn's 2.1 million LinkedIn Groups do not still hold value, but they are evolving. If a nonprofit has limited time to invest in LinkedIn, then LinkedIn Pages are a much better option. In terms of groups themselves, if a nonprofit wants to organize small groups of staff and board members, volunteers, or activists, then Facebook Groups serve that function much better than LinkedIn Groups for the simple reason that staff and board members, volunteers, and activists are much more likely to be active on Facebook on a regular basis. However, and though its somewhat late in the LinkedIn Group adoption curve, creating a LinkedIn Group to reach those outside your network could be worth experimenting with. If your nonprofit's mission and programs specifically mesh with the unique character and demographics of LinkedIn, then you may be able to create a group that people will want to join and participate in. It's important to understand that LinkedIn Groups grow very slowly in the first year or two unless you promote them heavily on all your communication channels. Of all the tools available to nonprofits today, it's difficult to encourage nonprofits to invest the time in creating and promoting a new LinkedIn Group unless the nonprofit has a mission and programs that specifically match the interests of LinkedIn users, such as business development, marketing, corporate social responsibility, philanthropy, education, social enterprise, workforce training, employment, and so on. If you decide that a LinkedIn Group is a good fit for your organization or if you already have a LinkedIn Group, know that being an attentive group manager is essential for the success of your group as well as following long-standing group management best practices, such as:

- Create a set of group rules in your management panel that details specific guidelines for posting discussions and promotions and clarifies that spammers will be removed. At least once a month rotate a featured discussion created by the group manager that reiterates the group rules. You'll discover that doing so is highly appreciated by your group members.

- Keep your group a closed group that requires approval to join and be sure to set up the templates for the emails that are sent to prospective members when they request to join as well as when they are approved. Always include your nonprofit's website link in your template emails to increase referral traffic. Closed groups also make it more difficult for spammers to get access to your group. Quite often members who do not have pictures and connections are spam accounts, and their requests to join should be denied.

- Don't only feature your nonprofit's discussions as "Manager's Choice." Group members expect balanced and fair group management.

- Send bimonthly announcements that feature top discussions and occasionally a call to action for your nonprofit. Again, overmarketing on LinkedIn is a turnoff, so rather than using your group solely as a marketing tool, use it to foster community around your cause.

- If you name your group the name of your nonprofit and few people join, then consider renaming it something more general to appeal to a wider audience. People are often more likely to join a cause than a nonprofit, and fortunately you can change your group name up to five times until you settle on one that maximizes your member growth rate.

- On a quarterly basis share your group stats with your members so they can get a good understanding of who joins and participates in the group.

LINKEDIN PROFILES

The power of LinkedIn profiles for nonprofit staff and their careers is well-documented. When applying for jobs, more than 93 percent of recruiters visit a potential candidate's LinkedIn profile.[1] And as mentioned earlier, every activity that your staff engage in on LinkedIn is a direct reflection of their current employer—your nonprofit. The value of your staff using LinkedIn profiles is high enough that they should even be encouraged to be active on LinkedIn during work hours. Although you cannot demand that staff use LinkedIn, you can strongly suggest that they do so and give them guidelines for maximizing their LinkedIn profiles and activity, such as:

- Ensure their profiles are 100 percent complete and upload a professional photo.

- List all current and past positions as well as education.

- Upload work examples such as SlideShare presentations, videos, or crowdfunding campaigns.

- Give recommendations to get recommendations. Setting a monthly goal of recommending two current or previous coworkers, partners, and funders will result in your staff receiving more recommendations in return.

- Be generous with endorsing the skills of others as endorsements are often reciprocated.

- List all languages spoken, awards given, and publications.

- Join and participate in groups relevant to your nonprofit's mission and programs. While it may not be a good time investment to create a new group for your nonprofit, participating in large groups that already exist and sharing resources that link to your website or blog has proven to result in significant referral traffic. Like all social media, however, the trick is to post and engage authentically to avoid being viewed as an overzealous marketer.

- Follow your nonprofit's LinkedIn Page and like and comment on updates.

NONPROFITS TO STUDY AND LEARN FROM

❏ United Nations Development Program (UNDP): linkedin.com /company/undp

❏ Public Broadcasting Service (PBS): linkedin.com/company/public -broadcasting-service

❏ Program for Appropriate Technology in Health (PATH): linkedin .com/company/path

❏ Conservation International: linkedin.com/company/conservation -international

❏ Environmental Defense Fund: linkedin.com/company/environmental -defense

13

YouTube

Owned by Google and launched in 2005, YouTube receives more than 1 billion unique visitors each month of which 25 percent are mobile.[1] YouTube dwarfs any other online video service with 100 hours of video uploaded every minute.[2] For nonprofits that create video as part of their content strategy, YouTube should be the primary tool for hosting your videos. The tool set is comprehensive, and YouTube's Nonprofit Program offers additional services tailored for the nonprofit sector. Also, when you consider that 82 percent of all TVs sold by 2017 will be smart TVs,[3] YouTube's current smart TV-optimized design and smart TV apps position the company to be the leader of video consumption on smart TVs.

Nonprofits that currently create high-quality video content are positioning themselves for a future Internet that will be heavily reliant on the use of video to communicate stories and sell products online. The challenge today is that most nonprofits lack staff knowledgeable in video production or the financial resources to outsource their video campaigns. However, provided that you don't expect your videos to receive tens or hundreds of thousands of views, your nonprofit can still produce its own videos by interviewing communities served, staff, and donors, and by recording events and important program milestones. The person in charge of creating the videos needs to be creative, comfortable behind a camera, and skilled in video editing software. Much of your video content can be made using a smartphone or tablet, thus eliminating the need to purchase expensive recording equipment and accessories. You can also purchase high-quality and visually compelling stock video from services like VideoBlocks (videoblocks.com) and Pond5 (pond5.com). If your nonprofit decides to make video a high priority in your content strategy, it's wise to invest in video production training, such as low-cost webinars offered by Videomaker (videomaker.com) or in hands-on training offered by See3 Communications (see3.com). For inspiration, it's also a best practice to study the winning videos of the Annual DoGooder Video Awards (youtube.com/nonprofitvideoawards) and subscribe to the YouTube channels of large nonprofits similar to yours in mission and programs that create good video content to gain a better understanding of what kind of video storylines donors and supporters respond to.

It's worth reiterating that creating a consistent stream of video content in-house is very challenging for most nonprofits, and your time and resources may be better spent elsewhere. If you have a staff person capable and inspired to create video content, consider yourself very fortunate. Having realistic expectations from the start will limit the disappointment that often follows when nonprofits realize how difficult it can be for a video to surpass 500 views. The good news is that even if your nonprofit cannot create quality video content on a regular basis, you can still supplement your YouTube channel by curating quality videos not created by your nonprofit, but relevant to your mission and programs.

YOUTUBE FOR FUNDRAISING AND CAUSE AWARENESS

Through YouTube's Nonprofit Program, your nonprofit can add a Google Wallet donate button to the homepage of your YouTube channel and on the right-hand side of all your videos on individual video pages. Thus far YouTube has not released any data on how much has been raised through its digital wallet service. The results are likely to be minimal thus far, but once digital wallets go mainstream, YouTube could become a powerful driver of online donations. Investing the time to sign up for

YouTube's Nonprofit Program is time well spent. However, understand that currently the power of YouTube for fundraising and cause awareness is in using video to better tell your nonprofit's story. Video storytelling is not a fundraising strategy in and of itself, but when integrated into your overall fundraising strategy and campaigns, video storytelling has proved to inspire donors and supporters to give and take action. When polled in 2013, online donors responded that reading a compelling story is what most often triggers their online giving, but watching an inspiring online video was a close second.[4]

TOP FIVE YOUTUBE
BEST PRACTICES FOR NONPROFITS

Sadly, too many nonprofits neglect their YouTube channels by not investing an hour or two exploring and experimenting with the YouTube tool set. The approach taken thus far by most nonprofits is to simply log in, upload their video, and log out as quickly as possible. This upload-and-run approach is obvious if you spend a couple of minutes browsing nonprofit YouTube channels. The majority are not branded and are absent of "About" information. Videos are poorly titled, and video descriptions are often too short and riddled with spelling and grammatical mistakes. If nonprofits committed more time to researching the YouTube tool set, they would undoubtedly be surprised to discover that YouTube offers built-in video editing software and analytics as well as extensive social sharing and social networking functionalities—all of which are updated on a regular basis.

1. Maximize Your YouTube Channel Description

Your YouTube channel description should be short and should include a link to your nonprofit's website and social networks. The current design automatically displays the links in an icon format on your channel's home page. Additionally, you may want to add two or three powerful stats that speak to your mission and programs.

2. Title Videos to Increase SEO

YouTube is the second largest search engine (bigger than Bing, Yahoo!, and ASK combined[5]), and to maximize your YouTube SEO, your nonprofit should invest much thought into crafting titles for your videos. When you conduct a search on YouTube, video titles are heavily prioritized in search results. Use keywords in titles that are relevant to your mission and programs. If your nonprofit is locally based, then occasionally use the name of your city and state in your titles. It's also wise to include your nonprofit's name in your video titles. After video titles, video descriptions rank the second highest in YouTube search results. Each video description should be at least two or three sentences, and, unknown to many nonprofits, you can also add links to your video descriptions. Finally, be sure to use the tagging function to add keywords to each video.

3. Create Introduction and Closing Slides

Every video that your nonprofit creates should include opening and closing slides of three to five seconds duration that are designed with your nonprofit's branding and tagline. The opening slide can include the title of your video, while the closing slide should list or link to your website and social networks. Introduction and closing slides can be easily made using any video editing software and can be image-based or simply a solid-colored background embedded with text and links and your nonprofit's logo.

4. Utilize InVideo Programming

YouTube's InVideo Programming is a hidden feature that most nonprofits have no idea exists. Located under "Channel Settings," with a couple of clicks you can embed your nonprofit's avatar in your videos for the entire length of a video, or for just a couple of seconds. Additionally, you can add a thumbnail of one of your videos to another video to help increase your channel's video view count.

5. Curate Good Video Content

By creating playlists, you can easily curate some of the best videos on YouTube that are relevant to your mission and programs. This strategy is especially effective for nonprofits that have a minimal number of videos uploaded to their channel. For example, a small food bank could create a playlist called, "Hunger in America," and then add the best videos created by Feeding America or No Kid Hungry about food insecurity to the playlist. The playlist could then be featured on your channel's home page. It may seem counterproductive to promote the videos of other nonprofits, but if the video content is powerful and relevant, it reflects well on your nonprofit and ensures that visitors to your channel are not disappointed.

YOUTUBE NONPROFIT PROGRAM

Launched in 2007, YouTube's Nonprofit Program (youtube.com/nonprofits) is available to nonprofits in the United States, Canada, Australia, Germany, India, Ireland, Italy, and the United Kingdom. Nonprofits outside the United States can sign up for the YouTube Nonprofit Program directly, but for U.S.-based 501(c)(3) nonprofits to qualify, they must first be signed up for the Google for Nonprofits Program. Once approved, the following functionalities are added to your nonprofit's YouTube channel:

- **Google Wallet donate button.** YouTube visitors can make donations to your nonprofit using their Google Wallet account. Your nonprofit can set the default donation amount as low as $1.

- **Call-to-action overlays.** Your nonprofit can add a pop-up message to the bottom of your videos, which can include links to your website's donate page, social networks, or online petitions, for example.

- **Live streaming.** Using the camera on your PC or YouTube's mobile apps, your nonprofit can stream live events such as conferences, interviews, and meetings.

- **Video annotations.** With a couple of clicks, your nonprofit can add pop-up messages to your videos that can link to other websites. You can customize your videos to include multiple annotations throughout your videos in different colors and time duration.

NONPROFITS TO STUDY AND LEARN FROM

❑ WITNESS: youtube.com/witness

❑ Museum of Modern Art (MoMA): youtube.com/ momavideos

❑ Big Cat Rescue: youtube.com/user/bigcatrescue

❑ Anaheim Ballet: youtube.com/anaheimballet

❑ American Society for the Prevention of Cruelty to Animals (ASPCA): youtube.com/aspca

14

Pinterest, Instagram, and Tumblr

The growing popularity of Pinterest, Instagram, and Tumblr represents the dramatic shift away from text-based content to visual content. Pinterest, launched in 2009, reached 10 million users faster than any website in history, and it is fast approaching 100 million users. Instagram, launched in 2010, is a mobile-based social network likely to surpass 250 million users in 2014. And Tumblr, launched in 2007, is a microblogging site that hosts over 150 million blogs and has more than 200 million users. Different from other social networks, Pinterest, Instagram, and Tumblr require nonprofits to tell their stories and motivate donors and supporters primarily through images, and in truth, most nonprofits struggle to do so effectively. To build thriving communities on these sites, your new media manager will have to expand beyond the initial impulse to focus on marketing on Pinterest, Instagram, and Tumblr—that is, uploading donate buttons, annual reports, and photos of staff and volunteers, and instead tap into their most forward-thinking creative instincts.

PINTEREST, INSTAGRAM, AND TUMBLR FOR FUNDRAISING AND CAUSE AWARENESS

When used correctly, Pinterest, Instagram, and Tumblr can be very powerful for creating cause awareness. Compelling images evoke a much stronger reaction in online supporters and activists than text does. For fundraising, however, there are no data to prove that Pinterest, Instagram, and Tumblr help nonprofits raise more money than other sites, but the potential is there. Once nonprofits learn how to use the sites more effectively and as the tool sets themselves improve, it's possible that these sites will evolve and become integral to mobile and social media fundraising campaigns. Facebook and Twitter didn't begin to reveal themselves as powerful fundraising tools until 2012, but that didn't stop nonprofits from becoming active on Facebook and Twitter in the years before. And it shouldn't stop nonprofits that have the capacity to do so from experimenting with Pinterest, Instagram, and Tumblr. At the very least, Pinterest, Instagram, and Tumblr are excellent hands-on training tools for new media managers to become more adept at using images for storytelling. If an image is highly pinned on Pinterest, liked on Instagram, and reblogged on Tumblr, then it is guaranteed to also be popular on other social networks.

TOP FIVE PINTEREST BEST PRACTICES FOR NONPROFITS

Pinterest can be a powerful driver of referral traffic and has great potential for fundraising and cause awareness. The challenge, however, is to frame your visual storytelling in a way that triggers the impulse in your followers to repin and like your pins. If your nonprofit is uploading and repinning images that are consistently met with silence, then you have to dramatically alter how you are using Pinterest. Pinterest users often communicate that the attraction to Pinterest is seeing beautiful and inspirational images. In interviews, many Pinterest users claim the site to be a mental vacation from other online media where sensational and negative news stories and images are dominant. Pinterest users respond to images that make them feel good. Environmental and animal welfare organizations are an obvious fit for Pinterest. Beautiful landscapes and majestic wildlife images are some of the most repinned images on Pinterest. Food, fashion, travel, and art organizations are also well-suited to Pinterest.

Delicious and healthy recipes, fair trade clothing and accessories, international volunteer destinations, and eye-catching art all make for a successful Pinterest strategy. However, for nonprofits whose mission and programs focus upon the plight of human suffering, such as human rights, poverty, or antiviolence organizations, it's a much greater challenge to use Pinterest effectively since people do not respond to depressing images on Pinterest.

1. Build Your Boards Slowly

The central idea behind Pinterest is to upload and repin images to boards. Boards can be titled and described by theme, such as "Elephant Conservation," "Healthy Recipes," and "Inspirational Quotes." The current limit is 350 boards. However, nonprofits shouldn't begin their Pinterest strategy with more than 10 boards. You are much more likely to gain followers who follow all your boards if you have 10 or fewer. By initially creating more than 10 boards, you risk that your followers may choose to only follow a small selection of your boards which ultimately means less exposure of your pins. In time, as you gain a better understanding of using Pinterest, you can create additional boards themed for specific campaigns, such as a cause awareness day campaign. Your nonprofit should also arrange its boards on its Pinterest profile so that the most popular boards are featured at the top.

One of the most common mistakes nonprofits make when they are new to Pinterest is uploading 20 or 30 images to their boards at once. Instead, upload your images over days or weeks to avoid cluttering the home feed of your followers. Even though you can repin your own pins, many nonprofits do not realize this. If they have uploaded their best images all at once at the launch of their Pinterest profile, then they've exhausted their best visual content. The goal is not to build your boards quickly, but rather to build the best boards you can over time to maximize repins and thus gain new followers. If you upload multiple pins per hour, your repin rate drops significantly. Also, when creating your boards, know that board titles and descriptions are heavily prioritized in search engine results. Too many nonprofits rush to create their boards and give their boards names and descriptions that lack creativity and are not optimized for SEO. If this is the case with your nonprofit, you must backtrack and take the time to set up your boards correctly. Finally, be sure to set the most visually compelling pins as the cover photos for each of your boards so your Pinterest profile makes a good first impression.

2. Pin Content That Is Visually Appealing

Before you start pinning regularly, you should study which pins are getting repinned and liked in large numbers. Taking a couple of days to study Pinterest before becoming active on Pinterest will illuminate what types of images pinners respond to, and more importantly, what type they don't. Even if at first your nonprofit doesn't seem to be an obvious fit for Pinterest, some creative thinking may reveal a strategy. For example, an international development organization could pin recipes indigenous to the countries where they work. A health organization could pin healthy recipes and exercise tips represented by appealing food images and yoga or exercise infographics. An education organization could pin images of popular children's books, back-to-school outfits, and education infographics. And all nonprofits, no matter their mission and programs, should pin inspirational quotes and powerful stats in visual format since they are consistently the most repinned and liked images on Pinterest. You can use your own images and photo-editing software to add the text to your images or tools such as Quozio (quozio.com) and Pinwords (pinwords.com). Once you gain a good understanding of what motivates the Pinterest community, you'll likely find yourself creating and pinning content that you never would have imagined just a few years ago.

3. Ensure That Every Pin Links to a Website

Many nonprofits pin their own website or blog to ensure that their pins link directly back to their website or blog. This is a smart strategy because your analytics will often reveal that a surprising amount of referral traffic comes from Pinterest, especially if you have more than 2,500 followers. Rather than pinning directly from your website or blog, it's often better to upload an image directly to Pinterest and then edit the pin manually to include the link because images pinned from websites and blogs tend to be much smaller than those uploaded directly. It's an extra step in your Pinterest strategy, but if the images are visually powerful, it's worth the extra step to upload larger versions of your images in order to make them more eye-catching and thus repinnable.

When pinning and repinning images, you should always check the link attached to the image. Many pins go to unrelated sites, and others don't link to an external site at all which many Pinterest users find annoying. It's tragic how many nonprofits upload images that do not link to their website or blog (or Facebook Page, Twitter account, YouTube channel, etc.), thus undermining Pinterest's power to drive referral traffic. To track how many pins link to your website, enter "pinterest.com /source/yourwebsiteURL" into your browser. Finally, it's worth noting that 21 percent of Pinterest users have bought something they saw on Pinterest,[1] so if your nonprofit has an online store, be sure to create a board of your products and consistently integrate the promotion of your products with your Pinterest strategy.

4. Include a Short Description with Each Pin

When uploading an image or repinning, your nonprofit should always include a short description because pin description text is highly favored in Pinterest search results. Descriptions should be no more than a sentence in length. Multiple sentences or paragraphs show up as tiny blocks of unreadable text attached to your pins which can deflect attention away from your images. Also, when relevant, include hashtags in your pin descriptions.

5. Pin a Minimum of Twice Daily

At the minimum, your Pinterest strategy requires pinning and repinning at least twice daily, but not two pins simultaneously. Rather, your nonprofit should pin and repin throughout the day. If you have more time, add a pin or repin every two hours. Frequency of pinning is very similar to tweeting in that pinning every two hours is often enough to consistently engage your Pinterest followers, but not so often that your nonprofit risks cluttering their home feeds. To maximize engagement and interaction rates, prioritize pinning in the afternoon and evening. The vast majority of active pinners are women, many of whom are mothers. Therefore, their access to Pinterest coincides with their free time outside of work and parenting responsibilities. Similar to favoriting tweets on Twitter, to organize pins for future repinning, "Like" pins to add them to your "Likes" tab and once repinned, unlike them.

TOP FIVE INSTAGRAM
BEST PRACTICES FOR NONPROFITS

Owned by Facebook, Instagram is the largest mobile social network in the United States. With more than half its users outside the United States, Instagram is well-positioned to become more broadly used worldwide. The predominant age group of users is 18 to 29. At the time this book went to press, the Instagram tool set was limited primarily to sharing photos or 15-second videos, adding text-based captions, liking photos, and sending direct messages. The simplicity of the app is part of its appeal, but in terms of fundraising, nonprofits have few options for converting Instagram followers into donors. If in the future Instagram enables nonprofits to insert links into captions or attach them to photos and videos, then the app could become a powerhouse for mobile and online fundraising. Imagine being able to send your Instagram followers to mobile-optimized donate, text-to-give, or mobile wallet pages. That simple upgrade could instantly increase Instagram's relevance in your mobile and social fundraising plan. Until then, in terms of fundraising, nonprofits are limited to sharing images embedded with keywords and short codes.

For cause awareness, Instagram is a highly engaged community. Your nonprofit will likely receive more Instagram likes than Facebook likes and Twitter retweets combined, and it's a community that is very responsive to nonprofits and images and videos that foster social good.

1. Use Instagram to Report Live

When reporting live from the field or from events and conferences, your new media manager should be adept at using Instagram to capture moments and events in real time through photos and video. Always include a short caption, and like other social networks, inspirational quotes and powerful stats significantly increase engagement. When the event is over, you can convert the images into a web-based slideshow using Slidagram (slidagram.com) or a video slideshow using Flipagram (flipagr.am).

2. Share Screenshots of Photos

Using the screenshot function on your smartphone, you can add images to your smartphone's photo library that can then be shared on Instagram. You can create screenshots of your own photos or of branded images that you have posted on other social networks and then share them on Instagam. You can also share screenshots of compelling photos posted by others. When using images from others, be sure to tag them if they have a presence on Instagram using the "Add People" function. It's also worth noting that images embedded with quotes and stats are very popular on Instagram.

3. Add Hashtags to Captions, and Like the Photos of Others

Nonprofits that consistently use hashtags on Instagram have twice as many followers as those that don't.[2] Instagram users regularly monitor hashtags, thus enabling your nonprofit to gain more exposure to potential new followers. In addition to your event and cause awareness campaign hashtags, your nonprofit should also monitor and use the hashtags that are most popular on Instagram. Also, as part of your event reporting and cause awareness campaigns, you can crowdsource images and videos on Instagram by asking your followers to use your hashtag when sharing images on Instagram and then convert the images using your hashtag into a slideshow or embed them directly into your website or blog.

Another way to grow your Instagram following is to regularly like images posted by others. Each day take a couple of minutes to like at least 10 images posted by those you are following. In the future Instagram will likely enable users to forward their favorite images posted by nonprofits to their followers which will help your nonprofit gain new followers (similar to retweets). But until then, your nonprofit is limited to promoting your Instagram web profile, using hashtags, and liking the photos of others.

4. Use Third-Party Instagram Apps

There are a number of third-party Instagram apps worth experimenting with. In addition to Slidagram and Flipagram, your nonprofit should explore Statigram (statigr.am) for tracking your Instagram analytics and Copygram (copygr.am) which allows you to print your Instagram photos (good for volunteer appreciation gifts and as a fundraiser at events). You can also use PhotoGrid (photogrid.org) to create collages of your Instagram images and Pixlr-o-matic (pixlr.com/o-matic) for advanced photo editing.

5. Share at Least One Image Daily

To gain followers on Instagram, you must be active on Instagram. If possible, post once in the morning and once in the afternoon or evening. Instagram images and video have peak activity during the first four hours after sharing, so to be consistently active, you need to post twice daily. If you cannot be active that often, then sharing one image or video daily is enough activity to build a following slowly but surely over time.

TOP FIVE TUMBLR
BEST PRACTICES FOR NONPROFITS

Although Tumblr is primarily a blogging tool, it has many of the common features found in a social network. For your Tumblr presence to succeed, it's best to approach the site as social network rather than as a blogging tool. Although articles and traditional blog posts can be posted on Tumblr, the site's power resides in sharing visual content since large blocks of text are mostly ignored on Tumblr. For that reason, most nonprofits that have used Tumblr as a blogging tool have found it to be a challenge to inspire engagement and interaction. Also, Tumblr's ability to refer traffic to your website or blog is extremely limited. In truth, Tumblr is in dire need of an upgrade. The design and dashboard functionality are dated and confusing to many users. Bought by Yahoo in 2013, its continued growth is entirely dependent upon the direction in which Yahoo takes the site over the next couple of years. Tumblr's user base is 54 percent female with 67 percent of its users under the age of 35.[3] The site also has a higher proportion of Asian and Hispanic users than any other social network. If your nonprofit is looking to reach out to a young, diverse audience, Tumblr could be worth the time investment provided that your nonprofit has a large amount of quality visual content. Rather than creating a Tumblr for your nonprofit, you could simply create a Tumblr or numerous Tumblrs for cause awareness campaigns and events. For example, you could create a Tumblr exclusively for your annual conference or for an awareness day campaign, such as World Animal Day on October 4. You could still post content throughout the year, but instead of building the brand of your nonprofit, you build the brand of your event or campaign.

1. Purchase a Premium Theme

Designing a Tumblr is not easy. You'll need custom graphics and basic HTML knowledge. The vast majority of free themes are not good enough for nonprofits that are serious about building a community on

Tumblr. If your nonprofit is going to invest the time in using Tumblr, then it should purchase a premium theme. For less than $100, you'll have a Tumblr that makes a strong first impression and saves your new media manager countless hours trying to manipulate a free theme that is limited in functionality. Premium themes are modern in design and allow you to easily add e-newsletter and mobile alert opt-ins and social network icons.

2. Make Photos and Quotes a Priority

Photos and quotes receive five times the engagement and interaction rates than text, chat, audio, and video posts do on Tumblr.[4] You can upload photos and images embedded with quotes directly or use Tumblr's "Quotes" function. For photos, always add a caption, and include a link when appropriate. As a rule, for every five photos uploaded, use the quote function once and then intermingle your Tumblr content with video and the occasional audio post. Finally, Tumblr has a very well-built mobile app, so when you're reporting live, experiment with adding photos, quotes, and video and audio files in real time.

3. Reblog and Like the Content of Others

Curating good content on Tumblr is an easy way to be active on Tumblr without having to consistently create quality visual content. To curate effectively, you should follow a wide variety of Tumblr blogs. Reblogging also helps increase your following since your reblog is added as a "Note" to the original Tumblr post. In addition, similar to liking on Pinterest and Instagram, liking Tumblr posts also helps your nonprofit gain exposure on Tumblr.

4. Post Humorous Content

Tumblr is unique in that images and animated GIFs that convey humor are some of the most popular posts. You can upload humorous cartoons, images, and video and, when appropriate, you can use the quote function to upload humorous quotes and jokes. For inspiration, do an Internet search of "humorous images," "political humor," and "jokes" and follow the Working at a Nonprofit (workingatanonprofit.tumblr.com) and Daily Humor (daily-humor.tumblr.com) Tumblrs.

5. Post or Reblog at Least Once Daily

To gain exposure on Tumblr, your nonprofit needs to be active daily in order to gain reblogs and likes often enough to steadily grow your follower base. Similar to Twitter and Pinterest, Tumblr posts have a short life span because Tumblr users tend to follow many Tumblrs. Fortunately, the visual content you create for other social networks is compatible with Tumblr, so as long as you do not post the same content at the same time on the same day on multiple social networks, being active on Tumblr is not a significant additional time investment. However, posting two or three times daily will grow your Tumblr following more quickly.

NONPROFITS TO STUDY AND LEARN FROM: PINTEREST

❑ Wilderness Society: pinterest.com/wildernessorg

❑ Plan International: pinterest.com/planglobal

❑ National Committee to Preserve Social Security and Medicare (NCPSSM): pinterest.com/ncpssm

❑ EarthShare: pinterest.com/earthshare

❑ Cleveland Clinic: pinterest.com/clevelandclinic

NONPROFITS TO STUDY AND LEARN FROM: INSTAGRAM

❑ Water.org: instagram.com/water

❑ Surfrider Foundation: instagram.com/surfrider

❑ Oceana: instagram.com/oceana

❑ Los Angeles County Museum of Art (LACMA): instagram.com /lacma

❑ DoSomething.org: instagram.com/dosomething

NONPROFITS TO STUDY AND LEARN FROM: TUMBLR

❑ To Write Love on Her Arms (TWLOHA): twloha.tumblr.com

❑ Nature Conservancy: natureconservancy.tumblr.com

❑ Human Rights Watch: humanrightswatch.tumblr.com

❑ Gay & Lesbian Alliance Against Defamation (GLAAD): glaad .tumblr.com

❑ First Book: firstbook.tumblr.com

4

MOBILE AND SOCIAL MEDIA CAMPAIGNS FOR THE ADVANCED NONPROFIT

C reating good content and knowing how to properly format and distribute your nonprofit's content on mobile and social media are essential for your content strategy to be effective. However, for your nonprofit to excel at mobile and social media, more advanced knowledge is required. The nonprofits well-known for excellence in mobile and social media are expanding their use of social networks and embracing real-time communications and fundraising. As in the early years of mobile and social media adoption, the early adopters of rapid communications and crisis response are learning through a process of trial and error how to effectively play a role in the 24/7 news cycle and launch real-time fundraising campaigns.

Five years ago the concept of breaking news and reporting live was foreign to most nonprofits and was left mostly to journalists and media outlets. As the Internet's collective social conscience, the nonprofit sector and its donors and supporters have a unique role to fill during times of crisis. More than ever, the media now turn to nonprofits active on mobile and social media for information as crisis situations are unfolding, and they often include in their reporting how to donate to nonprofits that are responding to the crisis. Provided your nonprofit is skilled in rapid response and has positioned itself as an expert resource, then regardless of the scope of the crisis—local, national, or international—this informal but powerful partnership between the nonprofit sector and the media will continue to grow.

To be an early adopter, your nonprofit will need to hire a part- or full-time skilled new media manager who can also be a journalist for your cause and an online crisis response manager when the situation arises. Real-time communications and fundraising campaigns require a significant time commitment and an investment in highly qualified staff. This is true even if your nonprofit's mission and programs are not tied to crisis response. If your nonprofit wants to launch real-time fundraising campaigns and report live from events or while on location on a regular basis, you cannot expect current staff to also add these duties to their job descriptions. It is work that requires much planning, preparation, and a unique skill set. Over the next decade real-time communications and fundraising will become fully integrated into nonprofit communications and fundraising strategies. With the continued rise of mobile and social media and smart TV, it's an inevitable evolution. As always, those nonprofits with an organizational culture that embraces advancements in nonprofit technology will gain the most in terms of brand reputation and fundraising.

15

Real-Time Communications and Fundraising

The greatest challenge for nonprofits using mobile and social media is learning real-time communications and fundraising. It's a phenomenon unique to social networks, and few nonprofits have mastered the skill of reporting in real time. It's only those nonprofits that have a part- or full-time new media manager that have been able to position themselves as an expert resource during breaking news and on cause awareness days. To be effective, you need a well-informed new media manager who is on call and ready to respond rapidly when the situation arises. In the case of cause awareness days, the manager must be prepared weeks in advance and arrange to be one of the first nonprofits active on mobile and social media when the day arrives.

THE 24/7 NEWS CYCLE: BREAKING NEWS AND CRISIS COMMUNICATIONS

In the days of print news, a breaking news story that unfolds today was still headline, front page news tomorrow. On mobile and social media, breaking news is happening in real-time, as the story unfolds. Breaking news can be on an international or national level, or it can be happening in your local community. For nonprofits to tap into the power of breaking news, new media managers must be the type of people who are inclined to monitor breaking news on a daily basis beginning in the early morning, most likely on their smartphone on their way to work. To experience high engagement and interaction rates, your nonprofit must consistently attempt to be one of the nonprofits first to tweet, post, and share content related to a breaking news story that is relevant to your mission and programs—ideally by releasing and distributing a short statement on your website or blog. Real-time communications and fundraising require a fast-reacting journalistic approach to mobile and social media.

In terms of crisis situations, nonprofits whose mission and programs are related to crisis response and intervention must have a system in place so that they can respond quickly. Your donors and supporters will often seek out your nonprofit on mobile and social media while a crisis is unfolding to see how they can help and what you are doing to respond. If your mobile and social media profiles are silent on the subject or continuing to distribute content as if the crisis wasn't occurring, they are unlikely to seek out your nonprofit the next time a crisis unfolds. Nonprofits that respond quickly and consistently tend to raise the most money and receive the most media coverage and online buzz.

Nonprofits should also shift to real-time communications during important televised speeches, public policy announcements, and events. A perfect example is tweeting during the State of the Union address. The speech is ripe with opportunities for nonprofits to tweet about their cause(s) and calls to action. The hashtag #SOTU begins to trend the morning of the address and continues trending throughout the next day. However, because the address occurs in the evening, nonprofits have been mostly absent from the #SOTU discussion. Sixty percent of Twitter users access Twitter while watching TV, and 90 percent of online conversations about TV occur on Twitter.[1] With the rise of smart TV, tweeting in real-time during important televised events will become standard communication policy for many nonprofits by 2017. The sooner your nonprofit learns how to do this effectively, the better your brand recognition as a news source will be in the future.

Central to real-time communications is mastering the use of trending hashtags. Twitter is the best site for discovering trending hashtags. When practicing real-time communications on other social networks such as Facebook, Google+, Pinterest, Instagram, and Tumblr, all of which enable hashtags, use the same trending hashtag(s) consistently on all social networks. Twitter is *the* social network for real-time communications and your first priority. But during breaking news, crisis situations, and important televised events, you should update all your social networks. In terms of what and how to tweet, share, and post, your nonprofit should implement the best practices discussed for each social network in the previous chapters—excluding the frequency suggestions. When situations arise that require your nonprofit to shift to real time communications, you can post and curate content more often. You'll know when you are posting too much if your tweets are not being retweeted, your Facebook and Google+ posts are not getting shared, your pins are not being repinned, your Instagram photos are not being liked, or your Tumblr posts are not getting reblogged. All that said, large nonprofits with sizable communities have a distinct advantage in real-time communications because they have the possibility for greater exposure simply because of the size of their communities. If your nonprofit has more than 20,000 followers on any social network, having a crisis communications system in place is a must.

In terms of fundraising, crisis communications tap into two of the strongest motivating factors found in online and mobile donors—a sense of urgency combined with impulsive giving. Ensuring that your fundraising asks are well-crafted both in text and visual format is essential. For example, text giving as a result of mobile and social media peaks during times of crisis. You need to have a new media manager who can create a graphic embedded with your keyword and short code within minutes who is then also skilled in uploading the graphic correctly to multiple social networks while simultaneously managing and responding to their communities. It's a rare skill, and to do it effectively, all other job duties must be placed aside as the crisis is unfolding. Small and medium-sized nonprofits that do not have staff dedicated to real-time communications can still participate in breaking news, crisis situations, and televised events on a smaller scale, but raising a significant amount of funds will be challenging.

HOW TO TAP INTO THE POWER OF CAUSE AWARENESS DAYS

While embracing a comprehensive, long-term breaking news and crisis communications strategy is challenging for many nonprofits, all nonprofits, regardless of their size, can tap into the power of cause awareness days. Your nonprofit can create your own cause awareness day campaign or build one around those cause awareness days that already exist, such as Earth Day on April 22 (#EarthDay), International Youth Day (#YouthDay) on August 12, and World AIDS Day on December 1 (#WorldAIDSDay). Many of the international days are sanctioned by the United Nations. In addition, there are also popular awareness days that are national and local (search "awareness days"). You can also participate in the annual #GivingTuesday (givingtuesday.org) campaign which now raises an average of 50 percent more in total donations each year for participating nonprofits.[2] #GivingTuesday is the first Tuesday in December and coincides well with the year-end giving cycle. Your nonprofit may also want to experiment with creating your own giving awareness day in November or December, such as Valley Gives Day (#ValleyGives) created by the Community Foundation of Western Massachusetts.

Many nonprofits already participate in cause awareness day campaigns. Unfortunately it's without a strategy in place because most nonprofits aren't aware of the campaigns until the actual day of the campaign when they see other nonprofits tweeting, sharing, and posting about the campaign. To effectively use mobile and social media to raise funds on cause awareness days, you need to prepare months in advance. The first step is to decide whether your nonprofit will create your own awareness day campaign or build your campaign around an already well-known awareness day, or both. Then when planning your content strategy, add the awareness day campaign(s) to your editorial calendar. At a minimum, you need at least six weeks to prepare for an awareness day campaign. Once scheduled, to effectively promote and build excitement for your campaign, your nonprofit should:

- Create a page on your website that prominently features the date and hashtag of the cause awareness day and describes why the cause is important. It should also detail as least three actions that your donors and supporters can take on the awareness day, such as make a donation, sign a petition, share the page with their social networks, become a volunteer, and so on. This page should also prominently feature a donate button, an e-newsletter, mobile alert opt-in forms, and social network icons.

- If fundraising is central to your campaign, you can also create a crowdfunding project and/or a social fundraising campaign to encourage others to raise funds for your nonprofit during the campaign. If you do so, add a "Fundraise" button and pitch your awareness day campaign page.

- Consider hosting a tweet chat, Google+ Hangout, or webinar on the day of the campaign. Promotion for these online events should be integrated with your campaign page and included in all email promotions.

- Design a set of promotional images and graphics for your campaign in order to maximize promotion and sharing on mobile and social media. Be sure to embed your avatar or logo and the hashtag for the campaign on the images and graphics.

- At least one month before the cause awareness day, send out a save the date email announcing the campaign and ask donors and supporters to follow you on social networks so they can promote the campaign to their social networks on the awareness day. You should also encourage donors and supporters to subscribe to your mobile alerts so that they receive a text reminder on the awareness day. If you will be running a social fundraising campaign, encourage donors and supporters to create their fundraising pages in this email and provide a link to your fundraising guide. You should send a reminder email one week before the awareness day and again on the morning of the day.

- In the weeks and days before the awareness day, send out countdown tweets, updates, and posts on mobile and social media. Always include the campaign's hashtag and a link to your campaign page. You can also create a Thunderclap (thunderclap.it) to enlist your followers to help promote your campaign.

- On the morning of the awareness day, your first tweet, update, and post should announce that it is a cause awareness day. For example, "It's #WorldWaterDay! Help us provide clean water to the 780 million people worldwide who go without: yourlink.org." These are consistently the most popular tweets and updates on mobile and social media on awareness days. Post your announcement multiple times throughout the day for those in different time zones, but with different stats or powerful statements. If your audience is global, schedule these announcements to be sent throughout the 24-hour period of your cause awareness day campaign. Your announcement should also be sent in a mobile alert on the awareness day, preferably in the morning during working hours.

- On the day of your campaign, tweet and retweet a wide variety of content at least twice per hour and link to your campaign page and use the campaign hashtag as often as possible in your tweets. For other social networks, post two to three times throughout the day. Also, be sure to thank donors and supporters in real time on mobile and social media.

- In the days following the campaign, update your campaign page. Summarize the campaign's success and thank donors and supporters for their participation. In addition to fundraising totals, you could list the number of page views, retweets, and shares received as well as the number of petition signatories, volunteers, and so on. You should also announce the date of next year's campaign, if possible.

LIVE REPORTING: EVENTS AND CONFERENCES

Another form of real-time communications is using mobile and social media to report live from your events and conferences. To do so effectively, you'll need a staff person whose sole purpose is tweet, post, share, blog, photograph, record, and interview during the event. This person can't simultaneously serve as the event planner or volunteer coordinator. Reporting live requires undivided attention to do it well, and if it's not done well, then it's not worth doing. A barrage of marketing tweets and updates announcing conference sessions or superfluous observations and platitudes is not a compelling way to report live. To effectively document the event and engage those who are and are not in attendance in real time, much preparation needs to be done.

During the early planning stages of the event, before any promotional materials go to print or are posted on your website, you must select a hashtag for your event. The shorter the better, and if it is an annual event, include the year (#14NTC). Your hashtag should then be integrated into all promotional materials. Potential attendees will monitor the hashtag, and those attending will promote the hashtag on mobile and social media in the weeks and days leading up to the event as well as during the event. The more often people use your hashtag, the more exposure your event receives. In advance of the event, your new media manager should prepare a minimum of 10 tweets and 2 or 3 posts for Facebook, Google+, Tumblr, and so on (depending on how many days your event is scheduled for) to maximize marketing and fundraising results. When reporting is done live, marketing and fundraising content is often hurriedly posted in a format that lessens its effectiveness. So having it prewritten and ready to copy and paste when appropriate can significantly improve results. Your new media manager should also have digital copies of all promotional images and graphics as well as three to four that are created solely for uploading while the event is occurring. They can be branded images embedded with the event hashtag, quotes from speakers, or photos of the venue. Additionally, the new media manager should be familiar with the agenda, the list of speakers, and the websites for recommended restaurants and end-of-day entertainment.

On the day of the event, new media managers should come equipped with both a laptop and a tablet or smartphone that has photo and video editing capabilities and be provided a space where they can work uninterrupted. Live reporting requires new media managers to tap into their most advanced skill set throughout the day without pause. They will be juggling the management of multiple online communities while also listening and watching for event highlights to be summarized and reported on all the while toggling between a PC and tablet or smartphone and numerous mobile apps and web-based tools. For first-time nonprofit event reporters, it is a highly valuable learning experience, and with each new event their live reporting skills improve and become more beneficial to both their nonprofit and their long-term careers. To ensure that the live reporting of your event or conference is successful, new media managers should:

- Post only the most interesting quotes made and stats presented by event speakers. Listen carefully and be selective. The goal is not to repeat verbatim all that is being said, but rather to share the most impressive highlights. It helps to take notes using Word or a notepad during the presentation and then craft tweets and updates perfectly—correct grammar, spelling, and punctuation—before posting on mobile and social media.

- Write in the third person. People are following the event, not the reporter.

- Embed the most powerful quotes and stats on images and then upload them to mobile and social media.

- Use the event hashtag in every tweet, update, and post.

- On Twitter, don't tweet or retweet more than 10 times per hour or risk overcluttering the home feed of followers. On Facebook, Google+, LinkedIn, Pinterest, and Tumblr post only two or three times daily. For Instagram, upload a photo once or twice per hour.

- Throughout the day, photograph attendees and ask them to provide one statement about what they have gained from attending the conference and share their responses on mobile and social media.

- Conduct video interviews with speakers and attendees and host the videos on YouTube. Always include a video description and if possible, an introduction and closing slide (created in advance).

- Create a slideshow of the venue, staff and volunteers, and sessions with good attendance. Be creative and capture moments that are both serious and light-hearted and ensure that all photos have captions.

- At the end of the day, write a blog summarizing the day's events and incorporate photos and videos.

- Intermingle marketing and fundraising content with live reporting.

- Retweet the speakers and attendees that are also live reporting on the event.

- Throughout the day share links to the event home page as well as the event agenda. Announce new speakers by linking to their bio and headshot.

- If the event is several days long, share the blog summary as the last tweet, update, and post and let followers know what time the event begins and when live reporting resumes the following day.

Finally, and as a side note, if your nonprofit is ready to go mobile to eliminate expensive event and conference print materials, you can create a mobile conference app using EventMobi (eventmobi.com), Guide-Book (guidebook.com), and QuickMobile (quickmobile.com). The apps include detailed event and conference schedules, maps, polling features, photo sharing, and social sharing functionality. During the conference, promote the link to the app download page often. Fees start at $1,500 on average for large events, so be sure to ask for a nonprofit discount.

10 APPS AND TOOLS FOR REAL-TIME COMMUNICATIONS AND FUNDRAISING

To be effective in real-time communications and fundraising, new media managers need to be very adept at using mobile and social media on mobile devices. In addition to live reporting from events and conferences, they often report live while on location or in the field. If live reporting is an integral part of your content strategy, your nonprofit should add a smartphone or tablet, or both, to the annual budget. New media managers shouldn't be required to use their personal mobile devices for work. In addition to the must-have apps, such as Facebook, Twitter, Google+, LinkedIn, YouTube, Pinterest, Instagram, and Tumblr, below are 10 useful mobile apps and web-based tools that new media managers can use to bolster their real-time communications and fundraising efforts:

1. **Storify (storify.com):** Storify allows your nonprofit to document a chronological history of your events as they occurred on mobile and social media. Nonprofits can set up branded profiles on Storify and then create individual stories for their crisis response and cause awareness day campaigns, events, and conferences. The tool set allows you to insert tweets, videos, and images directly from your social networks as well as post links. Storify can be used in real time or at the end of your campaign or event to display a selection of the best mobile and social media content created during your campaign or event.

2. **Studio App (madewithstudio.com):** Studio is a mobile app that enables you to easily add graphics and text to your mobile photos. You can insert quotes, stats, or a keyword and short code for mobile giving. You can also crop and add borders to your images and share your images directly from the app to your social networks.

3. **Share As Image (shareasimage.com):** Share As Image allows you to highlight text anywhere on the web and then easily convert the text into an image. You can customize background and text colors, fonts, and text and image sizes.

4. **Magisto App (magisto.com):** Magisto empowers new media managers to edit video clips using tablets or smartphones. The functions are basic, but good enough for recording, editing, and publishing short video interviews in real time.

5. **EventStagram (eventstagr.am):** For nonprofits looking to crowd-source photos taken at events in real time, EventStagram enables photos uploaded to Instagram that are tagged with your event or conference hashtag to be displayed on a TV or screen provided you have access to a projector. Fees range from $50 to $300, and inappropriate photos can be blocked.

6. **Evernote App (evernote.com):** To help keep you organized, Evernote enables you to easily create and organize notes, images, and links as well as store documents and record audio clips. Your content can be organized into notebooks, and your Evernote account can be synchronized with your PC, tablet, and smartphone, thus allowing easy access from anywhere at any time.

7. **LiveStream (livestream.com):** LiveStream can be used to broadcast your events and conferences online in real time. Branded, ad-free channels start at $50 a month. You can either use their mobile app to stream live or invest in video equipment. If you don't want to broadcast your entire event, you can periodically stream live to broadcast short interviews with speakers, attendees, staff, and volunteers.

8. **Flipboard App (flipboard.com):** Flipboard is a mobile app that organizes breaking news and popular web content by category. You can easily flip through your favorite news sources and magazines and share articles directly to mobile and social media. It also has a "Charities and NGOs" section and the ability to curate content into web-based magazines.

9. **Square (squareup.com):** For nonprofits that want to accept payments on their smartphone or tablet at events or conferences, Square is the most well-known mobile payment system. There's also PayPal Here, Breadcrumb by Groupon, and Intuit GoPayment.

10. **Foursquare App (foursquare.com):** Foursquare is the most popular mobile social network built upon the concept of checking in and adding tips and uploading photos to venue pages. Nonprofits can create a business account and then an event venue page to allow attendees to check in to your event or conference. You can also offer special promotions for attendees who check in.

16

New Media Managers

The success of your mobile and social fundraising strategic plan is entirely dependent on who is selected to be your new media manager. Despite all the buzz about mobile and social media, it's not the tools themselves that are powerful, but rather the people in charge of managing them. If they are inexperienced in online communications and fundraising and not properly trained in mobile and social media, then success will be elusive. Your nonprofit could be active daily on multiple social networks, but if your new media manager is not aware of and implementing the best practices that ensure success, then it's time and resources wasted. At this point in the evolution of mobile and social media, an advanced skill set is required to effectively inspire your online communities to donate and take action.

10 MUST-HAVE SKILLS FOR
NEW MEDIA MANAGERS

In 2013 the number of nonprofits that hired part-time or full-time new media managers increased fourfold.[1] As nonprofits have gotten better at implementing multichannel communications and fundraising campaigns and improving their tracking and reporting systems, many nonprofits have come to the conclusion that creating a paid part- or full-time new media manager position is worth the financial investment. For very small nonprofits, this may not be true, but for medium and large nonprofits—or small nonprofits with a desire to grow their brand recognition and donors base—it's becoming widely understood that new media managers have a unique and valuable skill set. It's very difficult to find a new media manager that encapsulates all the skills listed below. However, if this person is willing to learn and if your nonprofit has a training budget, individuals who have most of the skills can eventually acquire all the skills necessary to ensure that your nonprofit can achieve the goals listed in your strategic plan.

1. Creative Thinking

Expert new media managers have the ability to anticipate the impact of emerging trends in mobile and social media. They voraciously consume nonprofit technology blogs and study the mobile and social media campaigns of other nonprofits for inspiration. They use their creative impulses to come up with innovative mobile and social media campaigns for their own nonprofit. Rather than feeling overwhelmed by the speed at which technology now moves, they are energized by it. Too often new media managers are bogged down by a strategy or content approval process that saps them of their creativity. They need to be given creative freedom and be trusted to act upon their instincts. Some campaigns will fail, and some will need revision. But it's only a creative new media manager who keeps current with emerging trends in mobile and social media that can launch campaigns that stand out above all others.

2. Good Writing Skills

Woe to the nonprofit that incorrectly assumes that a new media manager is a tech position. First and foremost, it's a writing position. The ability to tell a story that captures the imagination of your donors and supporters and consequently inspires them to donate or get more involved is a skill only found in those who enjoy and excel at writing and who are committed to consistently improving their writing, grammar, and punctuation skills as well as increasing their vocabulary. Knowing how to format text for mobile and online readers is also critical in a new media manager. Too often great nonprofit stories go unread because of a poor choice in font size, lack of bullet points, or the outdated use of all capital letters.

3. Experience

It's very common for nonprofits to assume that volunteers and interns can effectively manage their mobile and social media presence simply because they are young and came of age during the rise of social networking. While it's true that the millennial generation has adeptness and curiosity about technology, using mobile and social media to tell your nonprofit's story in an impactful way requires a well-rounded understanding of the history of website and email communications, online fundraising, and how social networking and mobile technology have become intertwined with all nonprofit communications and fundraising. Young volunteers and interns who are lacking in the longer view of mobile and social media can quickly advance provided they are mentored by experienced communications or development staff, or given access to quality training. If your nonprofit is lucky enough to find exceptional volunteers or interns, you should still consider paying them for their work, especially if they are recent college grads struggling to find a job. They will be more committed and make an excellent candidate for your new media manager position should your nonprofit decide to hire one.

4. Photo and Video Editing Ability

To effectively work with image and video content, your new media manager must be adept at using photo and video editing software. Cropping images, adding borders or text, and creating visually compelling slideshows are skills acquired only through practice. Video content needs to be edited and embellished with visual effects, animation, and audio. The foundation of effective photo and video editing is a creative eye and an appreciation of digital photography and video. Quite often, your new media manager is also the person in charge of photographing or video recording events and program milestones. Being behind the camera takes confidence and a familiarity with digital equipment. If the photos and videos are poorly shot, it will be impossible to create a finished product worthy of publication.

5. HTML Knowledge

HTML looks much more intimidating than it actually is, and all new media managers should be skilled in basic HTML. To add a donate button, e-newsletter, mobile alert opt-ins, and social network icons to your blog, for example, you need to know how to work with an HTML editing software. Quite often when working in an e-newsletter publishing tool or with a blogging platform, you'll need to go into the HTML view to tweak fonts, page layout, and image sizes. If your new media manager is not trained in HTML, then finding and enrolling in HTML training should be a top priority, and it is an investment that pays off instantly through increased online donations, e-newsletter and mobile alert subscribers, and social network followers.

6. Multitasking

A new media manager will often toggle between five to ten different social networks and mobile and social media management tools in any given work day. At the same time, she or he might also be creating content for a website or blog, crafting an e-newsletter, creating visual content, or conducting research. It's rare that any web-based activity lasts longer than 30 minutes. Rather, a new media manager's day is divided into five- or ten-minute intervals—five minutes posting on Facebook, ten minutes creating a Twitter list, twenty minutes creating a Google+ invitation, three minutes posting on Tumblr, two minutes commenting on Instagram, and so on. The ability to manage multiple communities and projects simultaneously without significant mental drain day after day is a rare skill. Some development and communications staff who have added mobile and social media to their already full job descriptions feel overwhelmed when only managing a Facebook Page and Twitter account, but a new media manager's sole purpose is to juggle multiple mobile and social media campaigns on a daily basis. To do it well, these managers must be exceptional multitaskers.

7. Flexibility

Mobile and social media are in a state of constant revision. Just when you have mastered a new functionality, it disappears and is replaced with another. New media managers have to be extremely flexible, rein in their moments of frustration, and adapt quickly. They cannot rigidly attach themselves to any current social network design or functionality because changes often occur overnight and without warning.

8. Knowledge

Exceptional new media managers are plugged into breaking news and current affairs on a daily basis—not because they have to be, but because they want to be. Odds are that your new media manager is the first to know when stories and reports related to your cause are breaking and gaining momentum online. When writing blogs or moderating discussion on social networks, new media managers need to be well-informed so they can back up their statements with facts. Because their knowledge base is representative of your nonprofit's public persona, they need to be allowed the time to read and research trends and news related to your nonprofit's cause. A new media manager should also be skilled in conducting online research. Rather than getting stuck and delayed by not knowing an answer to a question or a solution to a problem, they find the answer by mastering search engines. New media managers are a walking, breathing, tweeting encyclopedia of knowledge and thus exceptionally valuable to the nonprofits they work for.

9. Community Building

The ability to use mobile and social media to generate online ripples of awareness is a very valuable, too often underestimated skill. At the beginning of the rise of social media, effective community building was equated with being human and "joining the conversation," but community building has progressed beyond personality as the primary means of inspiring engagement and interaction. Nonprofits are not human, and unfortunately too often it's the grumps, egomaniacs, and Internet trolls that are joining and usurping online conversations. Community building is now more strategic and based upon proven best practices. Tweeting, posting, and sharing content that triggers a positive response in donors and supporters require a new media manager to take an analytical approach to community building. Of course, your nonprofit must respond to questions and pertinent comments on mobile and social media with wisdom and graciousness, but the goal of increasing engagement and interaction in online communities should not be to merely inspire conversation, but to also produce tangible results and help your nonprofit achieve the goals laid out in your strategic plan. Three years ago "the conversation" and "listening" were defined as the driving purpose behind utilizing mobile and social media. Now that we know that mobile and social media campaigns empowered by quality content are what increases donations, volunteerism, and event attendance, the strategy must come first. New media managers with years of experience will likely have come to the same realization and are more advanced in their community building skill set.

10. Leadership

A new media manager will often be a couple steps ahead of other staff members in terms of nonprofit technology trends. At organizations where change is consistently met with resistance, new media managers will have to have excellent leadership skills to move an organization forward. They need to tactfully, but forcefully be the advocate at their nonprofit for advancement in mobile and social media adoption and budget increases—including asking for raises when the time arises. A new media managers' job is a stressful one that can easily lead to burnout if the walls of resistance are strong and their compensation doesn't reflect their skill set as it grows over time. Also, as the online representative of a nonprofit, a new media manager has to be comfortable with expressing opinions publicly. New media managers are confident in their experience and knowledge, but not arrogant. This balance in character must manifest itself both online and at the office.

HOW MUCH TIME MOBILE AND SOCIAL MEDIA REQUIRE

The amount of time that a nonprofit can invest in mobile and social media depends on capacity. Small nonprofits that are not in a position to hire a part- or full-time social media manager should limit themselves to one or two social networks and place the highest priority on their website, email communications, and online fundraising campaigns. Mobile and social media are powerful, but when implemented on a small scale, the power is overshadowed by other more traditional online campaigns. Often small nonprofits try to be active on more than two social networks by sharing the responsibility among staff. While this is possible, it does require a concerted effort and cooperation among all staff that content be distributed effectively and consistently. There still should be one person who is given the directive to research and then communicate best practices as they evolve to other participating staff.

Medium-sized nonprofits at this point should be considering hiring a part-time new media manager or at the very least examining how job descriptions could be altered so that the communications or development staff who are currently managing mobile and social media campaigns can be given more time to fine-tune their skill set and experiment with new tools. The argument against doing this is that budgets are too tight and inflexible. Although this is a valid argument, where there is a will, there is a way. This book has laid out very clearly how mobile and social media will soon surpass PC communications and fundraising, and within the next decade it's very likely that print communications and fundraising will be used only intermittently in niche awareness and fundraising campaigns. Moore's law[2] concludes that 20,000 years of technological advancement now occurs every 100 years. Applied to nonprofit technology, the speed of advancement now doubles every two years. Your nonprofit is going to need a new media manager who can keep up with the pace of change in mobile and social media as well as with the tools that haven't been invented yet, but will likely affect nonprofits in profound ways just a few years from now.

Large nonprofits should have in place or be in the process of hiring a full-time new media manager. The volume of their website traffic, the size of the e-newsletter list and donor database, and their brand recognition all contribute to the argument that not investing in a new media manager would be counterproductive. The math alone of converting large numbers of website visitors, e-newsletter subscribers, and donors into social network followers and mobile alert subscribers is reason enough to hire a skilled new media manager who can then use mobile and social media to inspire donors to give more and more often and to enlist supporters to get more involved with your nonprofit. Some early adopter large nonprofits are hiring multiple new media management staff—one or two to manage social media campaigns, another to spearhead mobile efforts, and yet another to pioneer the rise of smart TV. The early adopter nonprofits have almost a decade of experience in social media and at least three or four years in mobile technology. The success of their mobile and social media campaigns has resulted in a significant shift in communications and fundraising priorities and thus budgets.

To make it relatively easy to craft a new media manager job description, bullet-pointed below is an estimate of how much time mobile and social media require. It does not include the time necessary for managing a website or email communications which ranges from five to forty hours weekly depending on your organization's size. If your new media manager is also meant to manage the website and email communications, then the times given below are in addition to the hours allotted weekly for website management and email communications. Based on the content and social networks that you have chosen to make a priority in your content strategy, you can adjust current job descriptions or craft a new one for hiring a new media manager:

- **Blogging (4 hours):** To write an average of two posts weekly which includes the time necessary to find, edit, and insert photos and integrate video.

- **Facebook (4 hours):** To post and schedule status updates four to six times weekly, respond to messages and comments, and monitor insights.

- **Twitter (4 hours):** To tweet and retweet an average of four times daily, to respond to messages and mentions, to organize followers into lists, and to strategically follow others.

- **Google+ (4 hours):** To share updates three to four times weekly, +1 the posts of others, and participate in Google+ Communities.

- **LinkedIn (4 hours):** To share two to three posts weekly, maintain your personal profile, and participate in LinkedIn Groups.

- **YouTube (1 hour weekly):** To upload video, create playlists, subscribe to other channels, and study the video campaigns of other nonprofits.

- **Pinterest (3 hours weekly):** To pin or repin images twice daily and maintain your boards.

- **Instagram (3 hours weekly):** To share one to two images or videos daily and like the photos of others.

- **Tumblr (3 hours weekly):** To post or reblog one to two times daily and like the posts of others.

- **Miscellaneous activities (4 hours weekly):** To create Facebook invitations, promote and host quarterly tweetchats and Google+ Hangouts, report live, and participate in awareness day campaigns.

- **Create graphics and visual content (3 hours weekly):** To design branded images, infographics, video, online presentations, and social network banners.

- **Research (2 hours weekly):** To investigate trends in nonprofit technology and monitor breaking news and current affairs.

- **Feedback (1 hour weekly):** To track and report on success.

To embrace all the job duties listed above, you'd need to hire a full-time new media manager. Even though 61 percent of nonprofits spent more time than previously utilizing mobile and social media in 2013, less than 2 percent invested more than 21 hours a week.[3] Thus, if your nonprofit is not willing or able to hire a part- or full-time new media manager, then you have to select carefully the social networks that your nonprofit can realistically and effectively maintain. For years social media has been considered free, so executive staff did not make necessary financial investments and consequently many communications and development staff now find themselves with many of the above job duties added to their list of job responsibilities, but without official recognition. This is an unsustainable approach to mobile and social media that puts a great strain on many communications and development staff.

In terms of time management, one very important point needs to be made about content creation and distribution: the content you create specifically for mobile and social media in any given week, such as blog posts, branded images, and promotional graphics, can be posted on all your social networks, but not at the same time. For example, in your editorial calendar for next week, let's say you are committed to creating two blog posts, one branded image with an inspirational quote, and one promotional graphic for your upcoming annual gala. The time required to create that content is approximately eight hours. You can then distribute the content throughout the week to your various social networks. For example:

- **Monday:** Post blog post 1 to Facebook and Twitter. Share branded image on Google+. Upload annual gala graphic to Pinterest.

- **Tuesday:** Upload annual gala graphic to Facebook and Twitter. Share blog post 1 on Google+, Pinterest, and LinkedIn.

- **Wednesday:** Share blog post 2 on Google+. Upload annual gala graphic to Instagram. Upload branded image to Twitter and Pinterest.

- **Thursday:** Upload branded image on Facebook. Tweet blog post 2.

- **Friday:** Pin blog post 2. Share annual gala graphic on Google+.

- **Saturday:** Post blog post 2 to Facebook. Upload branded image to Instagram.

- **Sunday:** Share blog post 2 on LinkedIn.

This method of content distribution maximizes exposure to your content and enables you to reach multiple online communities without having to create unique content for each social network. If you are posting the same content to three or more social networks on any given day, such as a blog post, then share the blog post on one or two social networks in the morning and on others in the afternoon. Then intermingled within this distribution schedule is content curation and repeat posting of content created in the weeks before. For example, the annual gala graphic should be promoted multiple times on each social network in the month leading up to the gala—in the mornings, afternoons, and evenings. As long as your new media manager is skilled in content creation and multitasking, your nonprofit can have a dynamic, engaging presence on multiple social networks with a relatively small amount of content. The time saved distributing content efficiently then provides your new media manager with the time necessary to interact with communities, experiment with new tools, track and report success, and plan long-term mobile and social media campaigns such as tweet chats, Google+ Hangouts, and awareness day campaigns.

HOW TO BUILD A CONSISTENT BRAND ACROSS ALL YOUR ORGANIZATION'S CHAPTERS

All medium and large nonprofits with multiple chapters eventually experience a unique, but common problem in their mobile and social media campaigns. Quite often their chapters create Facebook Pages or Twitter accounts before the state, national, or international office is ready to move forward with mobile and social media. Also common, the head office gives the green light to its chapters to create their own presence on mobile and social media, but now regrets the decision because the nonprofit's online brand is inconsistent, and in some cases, poorly represented. On the flip side, some head offices have chosen to not allow their chapters to have their own presence, but are now ready to move forward with a comprehensive, organization-wide mobile and social media strategy. Either way, large nonprofits with multiple chapters have much to gain by empowering their chapters to create mobile and social media communities tailored for their local area provided that they are done well and with much preparation.

In the cases where the head office has to rein in the chapters, it is much more complicated. It's common for the chapters to resent the head office's sudden intervention, and they don't want to lose their creative freedom and control over their social network communities. However, there's always room for improvement, and creating a consistent brand across all chapters and encouraging an organization-wide adoption of best practices benefits all parties involved. Chapters need to be open to expert direction, and the head office needs to provide valuable and useful guidance and easy-to-implement instructions. Doing so requires a significant time investment, but it can and should be done.

Step 1: Create an Email List of Chapter Mobile and Social Media Campaigners

The head office should create an email list of those who are responsible for mobile and social media campaigns at chapter offices. To successfully build a consistent brand across all chapters, the head office will need to be in regular communication with the chapter offices. If there is staff turnover, a system needs to be in place to ensure that new staff are added to the email list and that the old ones are removed.

Step 2: Create Avatars and Banners for Your Chapters

On the nonprofit's website, the head office should provide a downloadable version of the primary avatar(s) (200 × 200 pixels). If the avatar needs to be customized to mention a city, state, or country, provide a Photoshop file of the avatar for those chapters that have the ability to customize the avatar themselves. If they do not have the ability, then the head office must customize the avatar for them. Provide simple instructions on how they can submit a request for a customized avatar and give them a time frame for when they can expect the avatar to be sent.

While customizing numerous avatars may seem cumbersome, in reality it takes less than two minutes to add a city, state, or country to a Photoshop file. Avatars change only in the case of organizational rebrand, so if you do it once for all chapters, it will likely be years until you will have to do it again.

Additionally, the head office should design at least five different versions of banners and backgrounds for social networks and then upload them to the website for easy download. By providing five, you give the chapters a choice in how to brand their social networks. You should also suggest that they select and rotate banners at least three times a year. Five new banners should be designed and added each year. If last year's banners are no longer timely, remove them from your website and request that your chapters do the same.

Step 3: Create a Best Practices Document

In addition to avatars and banners, the page(s) on your website dedicated to creating a consistent brand across all chapters should also include (to begin with) the 10 most important best practices that the head office wants its chapters to implement. When best practices change or new ones are added, email your chapters. Always be helpful and of service and let your chapters know that they can contact the person in charge of the organization-wide branding effort, likely the new media manager, if they have any questions or concerns. It will help melt resistance. To lessen the likelihood of squabbles, source each best practice with examples and links to nonprofit technology resources that back up your enforcement of the selected best practices.

Step 4: Offer Training Through Webinars

At least twice annually, schedule a mandatory webinar (60 minutes or less) that demonstrates live the best practices. GoToWebinar and ReadyTalk are the easiest webinar tools to use. You should budget at least $100 a month for the month the training occurs if you need to train 100 attendees or fewer. For 10 attendees or less, use Skype Premium. Google+ Hangouts are free but not as reliable as the paid services. You should alert your chapters at least three months before the webinar is to occur that they should save the date. At two months before, send another reminder. At one month before, send them their log-in and call-in information. And of course, in the weeks before the webinar, send weekly reminders.

Step 5: Publish a Monthly E-Newsletter that Features Chapter Excellence and Provides Resources

Odds are that the chapter staff in charge of managing your nonprofit's mobile and social media campaigns on the local level are limited in their ability to research current trends because of time constraints. Thus, the head office should publish a monthly e-newsletter that features blog posts and articles related to mobile and social media best practices as well as customized advice for the chapters. For example, if the head office decides to become active on Instagram and it wants to recommend that its chapters do the same, then the head office should write a short article about how the chapters should create and configure their Instagram accounts and provide links to resources about how to use Instagram successfully. Also, each month the e-newsletter should feature a chapter that is excelling in its use of mobile and social media. Doing so demonstrates that the head office appreciates the efforts of the chapter offices and also provides an incentive for other chapters to excel in their use of mobile and social media.

Step 6: Create an Enforcement Policy

For the chapters that repeatedly ignore best practices and do not attend webinars, it needs to be made clear that an executive staff member at the chapter office will be contacted and notified to trigger a review process. If during the review process it is revealed that the problem is a result of the chapter not having the staff resources necessary to maintain the social networks effectively, then the promotion of all mobile and social media campaigns should be halted until a new staff person or volunteer is found to manage the campaigns. If the review process reveals that chapter staff do not cooperate simply because they do not agree with the best practices or resent the top-down directive, then a discussion needs to take place about a new staff person taking on the responsibility. Most chapters will see the logic of the best practices selected and appreciate the effort to train them to become better at managing mobile and social media campaigns, but occasionally personality conflicts occur that need to be resolved.

HOW TO BUILD YOUR ONLINE BRAND IN MULTIPLE TIME ZONES

Nonprofits whose causes are relevant to the global citizenry should make a concerted effort to be active on social networks on a 24-hour basis. To begin, you must become knowledgeable about the world's time zones. TimeandDate.com (timeanddate.com) allows you to easily view the time is in the world's largest cities. You can also enter "what time is it in [country name]?" into any search engine to discover the current time in other parts of the world. Half the world's population is most active on mobile and social media during your evening hours and while you are sleeping. If your nonprofit wants to build a global community or reach donors in other time zones, then you have to expand beyond your own location and time zone. In addition, you should also bookmark a translation website, such as Translate (translate.com) or Google Translate (translate .google.com).

For Twitter, you can use HootSuite, TweetDeck, or Buffer (bufferapp .com) to schedule tweets in advance. At the end of your work day, schedule one or two tweets to go out in the evening and early morning. For Facebook, use Facebook's scheduling function. Do not use HootSuite because status updates posted from dashboards score very low in Facebook's algorithm. You can use HootSuite or Buffer to schedule posts for Google+ and LinkedIn although at some point Google+ and LinkedIn will likely launch their own scheduling functions. For Pinterest, Instagram, and Tumblr, you are going to need a dedicated new media manager willing to take five minutes three to four times a week to be active when he or she first wakes up or in the evening hours, most easily done using a smartphone.

HOW TO RESPOND TO TROLLS AND DIFFICULT ONLINE PERSONALITIES

The rapid rise of mobile and social media has directly correlated with a rise in Internet trolls—individuals whose sole purpose is to rant, vent, and incite discord. Most users of mobile and social media have come to recognize a troll and ignore rather engage them. More often than not, the comments of trolls are relegated to the "crazy" category by your followers. Ironically, when considering the much buzzed about best practice of using mobile and social media to listen to your communities, quite often the most active personalities in your communities are those you should listen to the least. On mobile and social media, it's a best practice to listen selectively and give little credence to those who only post angry rants.

Those nonprofits whose mission and programs are related to controversial issues have to deal with trolls on a daily basis. But for most nonprofits, vitriolic trolls are rare. If your nonprofit experiences trolls regularly, by now you've likely come to realize that more often than not your communities will come to your defense and that there's little need for your nonprofit to get involved and waste time in an argument with a troll. Sometimes a response to a troll is called for. Your nonprofit should confidently reiterate your opinion with a link to an additional resource backing up your claim, but going back and forth with a troll is a complete waste of time and mental energy. If the troll attacks others or is just blatantly disrespectful or rude, don't hesitate to block or delete the troll from your community—except in the case where your mission is advocating free speech. But even then attacking others and using foul language is grounds for removal. Once they're blocked, you'll never hear from these trolls again. They are boosted by anonymity and will very rarely, if ever, follow up with a complaint via email or phone that they were blocked from your community. Allowing trolls to rant inside your communities can quickly contaminate your community and turn off your followers. Trolls should be dealt with swiftly and without regret.

Followers who disagree with your position, but do so respectfully, should be addressed and allowed to continue to be a part of your community. Initially, it's wise to practice impulse control and allow your community members to back up your position. Then post a simple statement recognizing their input, but again, stand firm in your convictions. Not everyone is going to agree with your position, and your nonprofit should not be afraid of, or give too much power to, those who disagree. That's the reality of the social web. Millions of opinions are now public, and some people more than others relish expressing their opinions online, even negative ones. However, it's important to focus on the fact that for every negative comment your nonprofit receives, your nonprofit likely has multiple likes and positive comments.

HOW TO MANAGE MOBILE AND SOCIAL MEDIA BURNOUT

New media managers often battle mobile and social media burnout. The mental energy required to actively engage multiple communities simultaneously is exhausting. Plugged in from early morning to late afternoon and early evening, many new media managers struggle to find balance at the end of the day when they need to shift their mental focus to personal and family responsibilities. Mobile and social media stimulates mental chatter and can sometimes even affect a person's ability to sleep. All day, almost every day, nonprofit new media managers are immersed in breaking news and thus the world's problems. Being constantly exposed to a barrage of new stories and images related to violence, poverty, injustice, and cruelty takes its toll. More than any other sector, nonprofit new media managers run the risk of losing their sense of hope if they do not take steps to effectively manage mobile and social media burnout.

The first sign of burnout is when managing communities feels overwhelming and monotonous. Good new media managers enjoy creating quality content and then gaging the response to the content on their mobile and social networks. But when burnout sets in, the focus shifts to reaching a minimal quota of status updates, tweets, and pins. The will to engage and interact is drained, and procrastination results. It's a natural response to an emotionally draining job, and the best cure is abstinence from mobile and social media. The brain needs a break from the barrage and needs to reset itself to normal operating mode. Taking a break from technology and the 24/7 news cycle is crucial. Many of the social problems we see daily have always existed, but it wasn't until the rise of mobile and social media that we were given constant access to the stories, images, and videos that document humankind's dark side.

Thus, when you go on vacation—and you must go on vacation—do not bring your work smartphone with you. You have to disconnect completely to be able to rejuvenate yourself. Let your coworkers know that you will be unreachable and turn on the "Out of Office" reply. If possible, don't even bring your personal smartphone. Overworked new media managers often find it challenging to connect face to face, or they cannot quiet their mind long enough to read a book on the beach or watch a sunset. During your vacation, you must relieve yourself of the problems of the world and reconnect with your inner nature. While you are gone, other staff can be given the responsibility of managing your mobile and social media campaigns. A community does not perish because of lack of activity for a week or two. It can be instantaneously reactivated when you return from your vacation.

You should also make an effort to schedule evening and weekend posts during work hours. Unless a crisis is unfolding, your evenings and weekends should be reserved for your personal life. Mobile and social media can be an unhealthy addiction that's too easily fed when your smartphone is with you at all times. Separating your personal life from work responsibilities is critical to maintaining a healthy balance. You should also regularly evaluate your physical and mental health. Sitting for 8 to 10 hours a day in front of computer, tense from being uber connected to your communities and the 24/7 news cycle, takes a physical toll on the body. Be sure to stretch and walk throughout your day. For mental balance, when you're offline read books, listen to music, and watch television programs that you enjoy. Also commit to seeing friends and family in person on a regular basis. Few recognize how difficult a new media manager's job is over the long term because it's such a new position, but once it has become your daily routine for a couple of years, the downside of being plugged in so intensely for extended periods of time begins to reveal itself. If not managed, you will start to experience compassion fatigue and body aches and pains.

Finally, mobile and social media burnout is compounded when compensation does not reflect your new media manager's skill set and time investment. Too many nonprofits are losing their most valuable staff because resentment is growing over low pay and overwhelming job descriptions. When polled on Twitter, less than 20 percent of nonprofit communications and fundraising staff have mobile and social media officially recognized in their job descriptions even though they spend hours daily on mobile and social media. This is a problem that eventually leads to burnout and high staff turnover. That said, the growing problem and phenomenon of mobile and social media burnout is also related to gender. The vast majority of nonprofit new media managers are female, and one of the main reasons why a gender wage gap of 19 percent[4] still persists is that women are much less likely to ask for a raise (or budget increase) and even more so in the nonprofit sector where financial sacrifice is equated with social justice work. Even small raises are better than none and can do wonders in retaining staff. With the average college graduate now retaining $29,400 in student loan debt,[5] if your nonprofit wants a skilled new media manager, then you must budget for one. In the long run, skilled new media managers will raise enough money online to cover their salary and then some, but it requires an upfront investment in salary expenditures.

ADVERTISING

For most nonprofits, mobile and social media advertising is out of the question because of budget constraints. You can experiment with a $100 ad investment on Facebook or Twitter, but keep your expectations at a minimum. Instead, perfecting the format of your tweets, updates, and

posts and creating visually compelling content often trumps financial investments made in advertising. For example, if a nonprofit uploads an
image as an update to Facebook and it is shared 100 times, then over the
next week the nonprofit can expect to gain as many as 500 new followers
as a result of the popularity of the update. For a Facebook ad to produce
the same results, you'd need to spend $190 per update because the aver-
age cost per new fan gained through Facebook advertising is 38 cents.
If your nonprofit has the budget, experimenting with mobile and social
media ad campaigns could be a smart investment during the year-end
fundraising cycle provided that the image and text featured in the ad are
visually compelling. Fortunately, the design aesthetics of mobile ads have
become less obnoxious in recent years and often function better as pop-
ups than flashing banners. Also, mobile advertising is expected to surpass
desktop advertising in 2017,[6] and early adopter nonprofits would be wise
to be one of the first nonprofits to create mobile ads that promote text-to-
give or mobile wallet fundraising campaigns. On a final note, in the spirit
of corporate social responsibility, the social network giants would also be
wise to offer free or heavily discounted advertising to nonprofits. Google
Ads did wonders for its brand in the nonprofit sector, and the same would
apply to Facebook, Twitter, LinkedIn, and so on. Ten years into social
media, it's surprising they haven't yet come to the same conclusion.

IMAGE COPYRIGHT AND FAIR USE

Hundreds of thousands of nonprofits worldwide break copyright laws
every day by uploading images and graphics to their social networks,
images and graphics they do not own, did not create, and did not get permission to use. Many nonprofits incorrectly assume that citing the pho-
tographer or designer of the images and graphics in Facebook posts,
tweets, and pins are enough to deal with copyright infringement, but
that's false. To be fully compliant with copyright law, your nonprofit
should upload only images or graphics that you have created, purchased,
or have permission to use because most legal experts advise nonprofits
to assume that all online images are copyrighted even if they do not have
a "©" symbol or a watermark.

However, Fair Use is a copyright doctrine that asserts that some images are public domain. According to Section 107 of the Copyright Act, "The fair use of a copyrighted work for purposes such as criticism, comment, news reporting, teaching, scholarship, or research, is not an infringement of copyright." It's goes on further to clarify that, "In determining whether the use made of a work in any particular case is a fair use, the factors to be considered shall include—the purpose and character of the use, including whether such use is of a commercial nature or is for nonprofit educational purposes." Thus nonprofits have some leeway in using online images in their mobile and social media campaigns. Are there absolutes? No. Each image and context of use is unique. Could you be sued for downloading a graphic from Pinterest and uploading it to Facebook? Yes, but it's highly unlikely, and if deemed fair use by a court of law, the lawsuit would not stand.

How your nonprofit chooses to use online images has much to do with your organizational culture. If executive staff fear the worst-case scenario, then your nonprofit will have to create all its own images and graphics, purchase them, or get permission to use them. If your organization is comfortable functioning in the gray area between copyright law and fair use, then the Internet offers an abundant directory of images and promotional graphics. Either way, research copyright and fair use law very carefully before making a decision. Worldwide, billions of photos are uploaded and shared every day on the Internet that are in violation of copyright law. And with more than 3 billion Internet users on the planet, it's much easier to educate artists, photographers, and designers how to proactively protect their work online than change the Internet habits of billions.

MOBILE AND SOCIAL MEDIA DASHBOARDS

Social media dashboards such as HootSuite can be very useful for managing and monitoring multiple social network communities, but there are downsides to using them as your sole means of distributing content and engaging with your social networks.

First, you run the risk of becoming more of a marketer than a story-teller. By design, mobile and social media dashboards are marketing tools most often used by other marketers—not your average donor or supporter. If you're not careful, you could become entrapped in a marketing approach to mobile and social media. The psychology of using a marketing tool by default tends to encourage a marketing approach to mobile and social media most often recognized in the tone and formatting of tweets, updates, and posts, or worse, through the mass automation of content. For many new media managers, the temptation to use a dashboard to post the same message and content to all their social networks at the same time is too great to resist, but doing so is the antithesis of being authentic on mobile and social media. If you prefer using a dashboard, it's recommended that for at least three consecutive days per month you switch to using your social network's websites or mobile apps so that you can experience how the majority of your donors and supporters experience social networks.

Second, emerging trends often cannot be detected when using mobile and social media dashboards. For example, the shift to native retweets becoming more powerful than tweets prefaced with "RT" was not evident in HootSuite. You also cannot experience how native retweets function on Twitter's website and in mobile apps inside Hoot-Suite. To this day many nonprofits are still using "RT" simply because they retweet only using a dashboard and have not updated their Hoot-Suite settings to "Use Twitter Web retweets." The shift to visual content is also much more noticeable when you use your social network's website or app because photos are much smaller in the feeds of dashboards, and interaction is not as prominently featured. It's quite stunning how different a social network's tool set functions inside a dashboard in comparison to their websites or apps.

As a general best practice if your nonprofit wants to be the first to notice and thus adopt upgrades to the tool sets of social networks, make it a rule to not be dependent upon using dashboards as they often lag weeks or months behind in updating their software to reflect the upgrades. Alternatively, new media managers can add social networks to the tool bar of their browser with the log-ins to social networks automatically saved. This allows for quick, easy access to your social network communities and without the risks that come with using a dashboard.

Finally, many nonprofits don't realize that the Facebook algorithm scores updates posted from dashboards much lower than those posted natively, and this is reason enough to never use a dashboard to post on Facebook. Some nonprofits insist on doing so because they can schedule updates in advance using a dashboard, but Facebook offers scheduling functionality as well which strangely most nonprofits have no idea exists. Perhaps it's because too many nonprofits have become overly dependent upon a dashboard and thus don't access their actual Facebook Page often enough to notice the scheduling functionality.

MOBILE AND SOCIAL MEDIA ANALYTICS TOOLS

Facebook, Twitter, LinkedIn, and Pinterest provide their users with extensive and free access to comprehensive analytics. Odds are that other social networks will eventually do the same. When tracking and reporting your mobile and social media success, using the analytics provided by the social networks is your best option. Most mobile and social media dashboards also provide free access to limited analytics as well as premium services for access to advanced analytics. In addition, you can use services like Sprout (sproutsocial.com) and Sparkwise (sparkwi.se) to access the analytics for multiple social networks. There's also Klout (klout .com), which provides an overall score for your mobile and social media campaigns, and Bit.ly (bit.ly) for shrinking and tracking specific URLs posted on mobile and social media. Your website and blog analytics are the most important indicator of your mobile and social media success and if not studied and tracked, then mobile and social fundraising success will remain elusive.

Your Mobile and Social Fundraising Success Checklist

Mobile and Social Fundraising Strategic Plan

❏ Conduct an online communications and fundraising audit.
❏ Organize a meeting to ensure organizational buy-in.
❏ Write a mobile and social fundraising strategic plan.
❏ Create a budget.
❏ Create a system to track and report on success.
❏ Implement your strategic plan.

Websites

❏ Decide whether to launch a new responsively designed website, to mobile-optimize your current site, or launch a separate mobile website.
❏ Select a Content Management System (CMS) and hosting service.
❏ Hire a website and graphic designer.
❏ Write content and secure photos for all website pages.
❏ Launch a blog inside your website.
❏ Prominently feature a "Donate" button and social network icons on your home page and every page of your website and blog.
❏ Add an e-newsletter subscription form to your home page and every page of your website and blog.
❏ Add social sharing and comment functionality.

❑ Select a website and blog analytics service.
❑ Get master copies of Photoshop files for all website and blog graphics from your designer.
❑ Configure your website and blog for search engine optimization (SEO).
❑ Test your website on multiple mobile devices before launch.
❑ Follow and study the World Wildlife Fund, Sex, Etc., Mercy Corps, Malaria No More, and Best Friends Animal Society.

Email Communications

❑ Select an email communication software.
❑ Design e-newsletter and email fundraising appeal banner images.
❑ Design e-newsletter and email fundraising appeal templates that are mobile compatible.
❑ Prominently feature a donate button and social network icons in your e-newsletter and email fundraising appeals.
❑ Get master copies of Photoshop files for all e-newsletter graphics from your designer.
❑ Add social sharing functionality.
❑ Create campaign-specific landing pages for email fundraising campaigns.
❑ Create an e-newsletter subscribe page on your website for effective promotion on social networks.
❑ Create an e-newsletter subscribe graphic to better promote your e-newsletter on social networks.
❑ Experiment with online contests to build your email list.
❑ Follow and study UNICEF, SOS Children's Villages, ONE Campaign, National Park Foundation, and the Electronic Frontier Foundation.

Online Fundraising

❑ Select a Constituent Relationship Management (CRM) system.
❑ Select an online fundraising software that is mobile compatible.
❑ Create a donate page on your website and ensure that the donation process occurs on one page.
❑ Set default donation amounts.

❑ Add an optional mobile alert opt-in field, if applicable.

❑ Add charity rating graphics.

❑ Include program versus operating expense graphics.

❑ Write and add giving impact statements.

❑ Include tribute giving as an option on your donate page.

❑ Create a separate donate page for tribute giving for effective promotion in email communications and mobile and social media.

❑ Design promotional graphics for your tribute giving campaign for your website, blog, email communications, and social networks.

❑ Create an ad for your tribute giving campaign for print materials.

❑ Include monthly giving as an option on your donate page.

❑ Create a separate donate page for monthly giving for effective promotion in email communications and mobile and social media.

❑ Design promotional graphics for your monthly giving campaign for your website, blog, email communications, and social networks.

❑ Create an ad for your monthly giving campaign for print materials.

❑ Design a "Donate Monthly" button for your monthly giving campaign and add it to your website and blog.

❑ Create a system to thank your monthly donors on a regular basis.

❑ Ensure that your thank-you landing page includes social network icons, social sharing functionality, and a thank-you video or slideshow.

❑ Ensure that your thank-you follow-up email is custom-branded and includes social network icons, social sharing functionality, and a thank-you video or slideshow.

❑ Create a "More Ways to Give" page.

❑ Create an annual thank-you and program achievement infographic or presentation and include it in your donor thank-you communications.

❑ Add your tribute giving and monthly giving campaigns to your "More Ways to Give" page.

❑ Follow and study Partners in Health, Feeding America, American Cancer Society, African Wildlife Foundation, and charity: water.

Social Fundraising

❑ Select a social fundraising software.

❑ Create a fundraising guide for your fundraisers.

❑ Offer contests that reward fundraisers who raise the most funds during the campaign.

❑ Create an email list solely for fundraisers, and throughout the year keep them updated on the causes that they raised money for.

❑ Create a mobile list for fundraisers and occasionally text them fundraising tips and event updates.

❑ Design promotional graphics for your social fundraising campaign for your website, blog, email communications, and social networks.

❑ Create an ad for your social fundraising campaign for print materials.

❑ Design a "Fundraise" button for your social fundraising campaign and add it to your website and blog.

❑ Add your social giving campaign to your "More Ways to Give" page.

❑ Send follow-up thank-you emails to social fundraising campaign donors with your nonprofit's branding and social network icons.

❑ Send follow-up campaign update emails.

Crowdfunding

❑ Select a crowdfunding software.

❑ Write your project summary and set up your crowdfunding campaign(s).

❑ Donate to your own crowdfunding campaign before launch.

❑ Design promotional graphics for your crowdfunding campaign for your website, blog, email communications, and social networks.

❑ Create an ad for your crowdfunding campaign for print materials.

❑ Add your crowdfunding campaigns to your "More Ways to Give" page.

❑ Send follow-up thank-you emails to crowdfunders with your nonprofit's branding and social network icons.

Mobile Fundraising

❑ Select a text-to-give software.

❑ Launch a mobile alert campaign.

❑ Add a mobile alert subscription form to your home page and every page of your website and blog.

❏ Add a mobile alert icon to your website, blog, and e-newsletter and email fundraising appeal templates in proximity to your social networks icons.

❏ Add your text-to-give campaign to your "More Ways to Give" page.

❏ Create text-to-give and mobile alert promotional graphics for your website, blog, email communications, and social networks.

❏ Create ads for your text-to-give and mobile alert campaigns for print materials.

❏ Sign up for Google for Nonprofits and Google Wallet.

❏ Follow and study the National Wildlife Federation, Humane Society of the United States, Human Rights Campaign, Greenpeace, and the American Red Cross.

Mobile and Social Content Strategy

❏ Write a mobile and social content strategy.

❏ Create an editorial calendar.

❏ Integrate mobile and social media into print materials.

❏ Integrate mobile and social media into news articles and press releases.

❏ Integrate mobile and social media into your blog.

❏ Integrate mobile and social media into image and infographic campaigns.

❏ Integrate mobile and social media into video.

❏ Integrate mobile and social media into online petition campaigns.

❏ Integrate mobile and social media into online contests.

❏ Integrate mobile and social media into your online store.

❏ Integrate mobile and social media into e-books and digital reports.

❏ Integrate mobile and social media into smartphone and tablet apps promotions.

Facebook

❏ Design and upload custom graphics to your Facebook Page.

❏ Optimize your page for Facebook Graph Search.

❑ Launch a Facebook Group, if applicable.

❑ Experiment with Facebook Events.

❑ Add Facebook Location to your page and request to merge existing Facebook Places Pages.

❑ Follow and study the Trevor Project, People for the Ethical Treatment of Animals (PETA), Doctors Without Borders, Amnesty International, and the American Civil Liberties Union (ACLU).

Twitter

❑ Design and upload custom graphics to your Twitter account.

❑ Organize followers into Twitter lists.

❑ Unfollow if you have mass followed.

❑ Host and participate in tweet chats.

❑ Follow and study Oxfam International, Natural Resources Defense Council (NRDC), Idealist, Gates Foundation, and the Acumen Fund.

Google+

❑ Design and upload custom graphics to your Google+ Page.

❑ Merge your YouTube channel with your Google+ Page.

❑ Optimize your page for Google Search.

❑ Experiment with Google+ Communities.

❑ Experiment with Google+ Events.

❑ Claim your Google+ Local Page.

❑ Host and participate in Google+ Hangouts.

❑ Follow and study Zoo Atlanta, New York Public Library, KQED Science, American Heart Association, and the American Association of Retired Persons (AARP).

LinkedIn

❑ Design and upload custom graphics to your LinkedIn Page.

❑ Add products and services to your page and request recommendations.

❑ Experiment with LinkedIn Groups.
❑ Ensure that all staff members have maximized their LinkedIn profiles.
❑ Follow and study the United Nations Development Program (UNDP), Public Broadcasting Service (PBS), Program for Appropriate Technology in Health (PATH), Conservation International, and the Environmental Defense Fund.

YouTube

❑ Design and upload custom graphics to your YouTube channel.
❑ Maximize your channel and video titles for YouTube SEO.
❑ Create introduction and closing slides.
❑ Utilize InVideo Programming.
❑ Create YouTube PlayLists.
❑ Sign up for the YouTube Nonprofit Program.
❑ Add a Google Wallet donate button to your channel.
❑ Experiment with call-to-action overlays and video annotations.
❑ Follow and study WITNESS, Museum of Modern Art (MoMA), Big Cat Rescue, Anaheim Ballet, and the American Society for the Prevention of Cruelty to Animals (ASPCA).

Pinterest

❑ Name, describe, and build your boards.
❑ Learn to brand and embed text on images.
❑ Follow and study the Wilderness Society, Plan International, National Committee to Preserve Social Security and Medicare (NCPSSM), EarthShare, and the Cleveland Clinic.

Instagram

❑ Learn to share screenshots.
❑ Add hashtags to captions.
❑ Download and experiment with third-party Instagram apps.

❑ Follow and study Water.org, Surfrider Foundation, Oceana, Los Angeles County Museum of Art (LACMA), and DoSomething.org.

Tumblr

❑ Design and set up your Tumblr theme.
❑ Prioritize images, quotes, and humor.
❑ Follow and study To Write Love on Her Arms (TWLOHA), Nature Conservancy, Human Rights Watch, Gay & Lesbian Alliance Against Defamation (GLAAD), and First Book.

Real-Time Communications and Fundraising

❑ Create a system to respond to breaking news and crisis situations.
❑ Launch a Cause Awareness Day Campaign.
❑ Experiment with live reporting from events and conferences.
❑ Experiment with Storify, Share As Image, EventStagram, LiveStream, and Square, if applicable.
❑ Download the Studio, Magistro, Evernote, Flipboard, and Foursquare apps, if applicable.

New Media Managers

❑ Hire a skilled part- or full-time new media manager or adjust current job descriptions of current staff.
❑ Ensure that volunteers and interns are trained in mobile and social media.
❑ Learn photo and video editing skills.
❑ Learn HTML skills.
❑ Build a consistent brand across all your organization's chapters, if applicable.
❑ Build your online brand in multiple time zones, if applicable.
❑ Proactively manage mobile and social media burnout.
❑ Get master copies of Photoshop files for all social network custom graphics from your designer.
❑ Study and mimic the mobile and social fundraising campaigns of large nonprofits similar to yours in mission and programs.

Notes

CHAPTER 1

1. International Data Corporation: Worldwide Quarterly Smart Connected Device Tracker, 2013: idc.com.
2. Urban Institute: Fundraising Effectiveness Survey Report, 2013: urban.org; Waggener Edstrom: Digital Persuasion Report, 2013: waggeneredstrom.com; Artez Interactive: Fundraising with Facebook Report, 2013: artez.com; mGive: Text Donation Study, 2013: mgive.com; Chronicle of Philanthropy: philanthropy.com.
3. Common Sense Media: Zero to Eight: Children's Media Use in America Report, 2011: commonsensemedia.org.
4. Pew Internet & American Life Project: Smartphone Ownership Report, 2013: pewinternet.org.
5. Millennial Impact Report, 2013: themillennialimpact.com.
6. #NextGenDonors, 2013: nextgendonors.org.
7. Pew Internet & American Life Project: Younger Americans' Library Habits and Expectations Report, 2013: pewinternet.org.
8. Blackbaud: The Next Generation of American Giving Report, 2013: blackbaud.com.
9. Pew Internet & American Life Project: Tablet Ownership Report, 2013: pewinternet.org.
10. Blackbaud: The Next Generation of American Giving Report, 2013: blackbaud.com.
11. Ipsos: "Reaching Today's Boomers and Seniors," online study, 2013: ipsos.com.
12. Pew Internet and American Life Project: Smartphone Ownership Report, 2013: pewinternet.org.
13. Nielsen: Introducing Boomers: Marketing's Most Valuable Generation Report, 2013: nielsen.com.
14. Dunham+Company: National Donors Study, 2013: dunhamandcompany.com.
15. Blackbaud: The Next Generation of American Giving Report, 2013: blackbaud.com.
16. Pew Internet & American Life Project: The Demographics of Social Media Users Report, 2013: pewinternet.org.

17. Pew Internet & American Life Project: Smartphone Ownership Report, 2013: pewinternet .org.
18. Dunham+Company: National Donors Study, 2013: dunhamandcompany.com.
19. Blackbaud: The Next Generation of American Giving Report, 2013: blackbaud.com.
20. Interview entitled "Is the Social Web Divided by Race?," produced by the BBC's Matt Danzico in 2012.
21. Pew Internet & American Life Project: The Demographics of Social Media Users Report, 2013: pewinternet.org; *Entrepreneur Magazine*: entrepreneur.com, 2013; Pew Internet & American Life Project: Civic Engagement in the Digital Age Report, 2013: pewinternet.org.
22. Dunham+Company: National Donors Study, 2013: dunhamandcompany.com.
23. National Center for Charitable Statistics: Nonprofit Almanac, 2012: nccs.urban.org.

CHAPTER 3

1. Webcertain Global Mobile Report, 2013: webcertain.com.
2. Mobile Marketing Watch: mobilemarketingwatch.com.
3. e-Benchmarks Study, 2013: e-benchmarksstudy.com.
4. Third Sector: thirdsector.co.uk.
5. International Data Corporation: "Always Connected Study," 2013: idc.com.
6. Annual Search Statistics Report, 2013: statisticbrain.com.
7. Public Interest Registry: Measuring .ORG's Trust and Success in Number Survey: pir.org.

CHAPTER 4

1. EmailMonday: Mobile E-Mail Statistics Overview, 2014: emailmonday.com.
2. Blackbaud: Online Marketing Benchmark Study for Nonprofits, 2013: blackbaud.com.
3. Blackbaud: Online Marketing Benchmark Study for Nonprofits, 2013: blackbaud.com.
4. Millennial Impact Report, 2013: themillennialimpact.com.
5. e-Benchmarks Study, 2013: e-benchmarksstudy.com.
6. Zarrella, Dan, *The Science of Marketing* (Wiley, 2013).
7. e-Benchmarks Study, 2013: e-benchmarksstudy.com.
8. GetResponse: Social Sharing Boosts Email CTR Infographic, 2013: getresponse.com.
9. EmailMonday: Mobile E-Mail Statistics Overview, 2013: emailmonday.com.
10. Network for Good Online Giving Study, 2010: networkforgood.org.
11. Network for Good Digital Giving Index, 2013: networkforgood.org.

CHAPTER 5

1. Giving USA, 2013: givingusa.org.
2. Blackbaud: The Next Generation of American Giving Report, 2013: blackbaud.com.
3. DonorCentrics Index of National Fundraising Performance: blackbaud.com.
4. Dunham+Company: National Donors Study, 2013: dunhamandcompany.com.
5. Network for Good Digital Giving Index, 2013: networkforgood.org.

6. Blackbaud: The Next Generation of American Giving Report, 2013: blackbaud.com.
7. Blackbaud: Online Marketing Benchmark Study for Nonprofits: blackbaud.com.
8. Blackbaud: Peer-to-Peer Event Fundraising Benchmark Study, 2012: blackbaud.com.
9. Blackbaud: Peer-to-Peer Event Fundraising Benchmark Study, 2012: blackbaud.com.

CHAPTER 6

1. mGive Text Donation Study, 2013: mgive.com.
2. text2give.com Mobile Trends, 2013: text2give.com.
3. Pew Internet & American Life Project: Real Time Charitable Giving Report, 2012: pewinternet.org.
4. Pew Internet & American Life Project: Real Time Charitable Giving Report, 2012: pewinternet.org.
5. mGive Text Donation Study, 2013: mgive.com.
6. mGive Text Donation Study, 2013: mgive.com.
7. mGive Text Donation Study, 2013: mgive.com.
8. mGive Text Donation Study, 2013: mgive.com.
9. mGive Text Donation Study, 2013: mgive.com.
10. mGive Text Donation Study, 2013: mgive.com.
11. Gartner: gartner.com.
12. Artez Interactive: Mobile Matters Report, 2013: The Impact of Mobile Technology on Peer-Driven Fundraising Campaigns: artez.com.
13. Compuware: compuware.com.
14. PayPal: paypal.com.

CHAPTER 7

1. Waggener Edstrom: Digital Persuasion Report, 2013: waggeneredstrom.com.
2. Waggener Edstrom: Digital Persuasion Report, 2013: waggeneredstrom.com.
3. Zarrella, Dan, *The Science of Marketing* (Wiley, 2013).
4. The Power of Kawaii Study, 2012: Viewing Cute Images Promotes a Careful Behavior and Narrows Attentional Focus: plosone.org.
5. Pangburn, Eric: "How Many Blogs Are There?," Snitch IM Blog, April 7, 2013: snitchim .com.

CHAPTER 8

1. Oriella: Digital Journalism Study, 2013: orielladigitaljournalism.com.
2. Hubspot: Introduction to Blogging E-Book, 2013: hubspot.com.
3. Waggener Edstrom: Digital Persuasion Report, 2013: waggeneredstrom.com.
4. See3 Communications: Benchmarks for Nonprofit Video Report, 2013: see3.com.
5. Slacktivism: wikipedia.org.
6. eMarketer Study, 2013: Smartphones, Tablets Drive Faster Growth in Ecommerce Sales: emarketer.com.

NOTES

PART 3

1. Forrester Research Report, 2013: How Consumers Find Websites: forrester.com.

CHAPTER 9

1. Facebook Statistics, 2013: newsroom.fb.com.
2. Waggener Edstrom: Digital Persuasion Report, 2013: waggeneredstrom.com.
3. Waggener Edstrom: Digital Persuasion Report, 2013: waggeneredstrom.com.
4. Millennial Impact Report, 2013: themillennialimpact.com.
5. Artez Interactive: Fundraising with Facebook Report, 2012: artez.com.
6. Waggener Edstrom: Digital Persuasion Report, 2013: waggeneredstrom.com.
7. AllFacebook: When to Post on Facebook: allfacebook.com,

CHAPTER 10

1. Blackbaud: Making Event Participants More Successful with Social Media Tools Report, 2011: blackbaud.com.
2. CNET: Twitter Founder Says Influence is in Retweets: cnet.com.
3. Computerworld: Researcher Cracks the Code on What Makes a Tweet Popular: computerworld.com.
4. Zarrella, Dan, *The Science of Marketing* (Wiley, 2013).
5. Ragan's PR Daily: Three Types of Tweets That Are Rarely Retweeted: prdaily.com.
6. Dan Zarrella Blog: How to Get More Clicks on Twitter: danzarrella.com.
7. Zarrella, Dan, *The Science of Marketing* (Wiley, 2013).
8. SalesForce: Strategies for Effective Tweeting Report, 2012: salesforce.com.

CHAPTER 11

1. Wired: Google Serves 25 Percent of North American Internet Traffic: wired.com.

CHAPTER 12

1. CNET: Heads Up LinkedIn Users: 93% of Recruiters Are Looking at You: cnet.com.

CHAPTER 13

1. YouTube Press Room: youtube.com.
2. YouTube Press Room: youtube.com.
3. Informa: Statistics on Smart TVs Report, 2012: informa.com.
4. Waggener Edstrom: Digital Persuasion Report, 2013: waggeneredstrom.com.
5. Jeff Bullas Blog: jeffbullas.com.

CHAPTER 14

1. The Next Web: 21% of Pinterest Users Have Purchased an Item They Found on the Site: thenextweb.com.
2. Dan Zarrella Blog: New Data Shows the Importance of Hashtags on Instagram: danzarrella.com.

3. Wishpond: Tumblr by the Numbers: wishpond.com.
4. Dan Zarrella Blog: How to Get More Likes and Comments on Tumblr: danzarrella.com.

CHAPTER 15

1. Advanced Television: 60% Tweet While Watching TV: advanced-television.com.
2. Chronicle of Philanthropy: Giving Tuesday Doubled Donations in 2nd Year: philanthropy.com.

CHAPTER 16

1. Vertical Response: Nonprofits Investing More Time, Money in Social Media: vertical repsonse.com.
2. Wikipedia: wikipedia.com.
3. Vertical Response: Nonprofits Investing More Time, Money in Social Media: vertical response.com.
4. Institute for Women's Policy Research: Gender Wage Gap Report, 2012: iwpr.org.
5. Institute for College Access and Success' Project on Student Debt Report, 2013: ticas.org.
6. eMarketer: Mobile Expands Its Share of Worldwide Digital Ad Spend: emarketer.com.

Acknowledgments

Thank you to my clients and all those who have taken my webinars. Without you I could not do what I love—or pay the mortgage.

Thank you to my mother, Diane, for your support while writing this book, and for always.

Thank you to Sarah—the smartest, most adventurous, and compassionate little girl I have ever known. I am grateful every day to have you in my life.

Thank you to my husband, Jason. You are loved.

Thank you to Gillian at Microsoft Citizenship Asia Pacific for giving me the opportunity to become a better trainer and world traveler.

Thank you to Maria at Bureau for Good for your generosity and hard work.

Thank you to the staff at McGraw-Hill.

Thank you to the wildlife conservationists. Mobile and social media have converted me into a donor and an advocate.

Finally, thank you to all those who follow and promote my blog and social network communities. I may not be able to respond to every kindness you express, but your retweets, likes, shares, +1s, repins, and reblogs are noticed and keep me inspired and committed to serve.

Index

About the Author

Heather Mansfield is the principal blogger at Nonprofit Tech for Good (nptechforgood.com) and author of the best-selling book *Social Media for Social Good: A How-To Guide for Nonprofits*. She also created and maintains the "Nonprofit Organizations" profiles on Facebook, Twitter, Google+, LinkedIn, YouTube, Pinterest, Instagram, and Tumblr which cumulatively have more than 1 million followers. Heather has 20 years of experience utilizing the Internet for fundraising, community building, and advocacy. To date, she's presented more than 100 social media and mobile media training sessions throughout the United States, Canada, Australia, New Zealand, India, and Southeast Asia as well as over 500 webinars to audiences worldwide.

Heather was honored as a "Fundraising Star of the Year" by *Fundraising Success Magazine* in 2009 and was placed on Twitter's Suggested User List from 2010 to 2012. She was also named one of *Time* magazine's Best Twitter Feeds of 2013 and currently serves as an honorary ambassador for the World NGO Day Initiative.

Originally from Springfield, Missouri, Heather moved to Los Angeles at age 19 to pursue a Bachelor of Arts in Political Theory from UCLA. Semester abroad programs led her to Mexico, Chile, and Argentina to study Spanish and anthropology. After college, Heather moved to Washington, D.C., where she worked by day at the Pew Center for Civic Journalism. At night and on the weekends, she volunteered with the Guatemala Human Rights Commission. Inspired by their work, she then moved to Guatemala to volunteer for Niño Obrero, a school for street children.

Upon returning to the United States, Heather moved to San Francisco. In 1999, Heather went on tour with the Lilith Fair Music Festival as a fair trade spokesperson for Global Exchange and upon returning became the communications director for International Development Exchange.

Heather's career in web and email communications first received national recognition when she launched eActivist.org in July 2000. She spoke at conferences throughout the United States and built one of the most popular e-activism websites on the Internet.

In 2007 she became nonprofit community manager for Change.org and shortly thereafter launched Nonprofit Tech for Good and the "Nonprofit Organizations" profiles. She and her family reside in St. Louis, Missouri.